Mentorship with Goddess:
Growing Sacred Womanhood

Kay Louise Aldred

Girl God Books

**Cover Art and Goddess Paintings
by Kat Shaw**

ISBN: 9798806863240

www.thegirlgod.com

Girl God Books

Re-Membering with Goddess: Healing the Patriarchal Perpetuation of Trauma

Re-Membering with Goddess is an anthology of women's experiences of trauma—trauma as a result of patriarchy; trauma perpetuated by patriarchy; and how through personal healing of trauma the Goddess is re-membered, re-embodied and resurrected. As repeating loops of trauma restriction are released—in the mind, body and nervous system—Goddess is re-embodied and rises... and the patriarchy falls.

Just as I Am: Hymns Affirming the Divine Female

What is a Hermnal? It's the collective sigh of our ancestral Grandmothers. It's a means of drawing us closer together as Sisters. It is a compilation of songs that affirms our Sacredness, apart from Man, and assures us that we are Sovereign Beings and Creatrixes, too. And it is our Love Gift of Gratitude to Mama.

In Defiance of Oppression – The Legacy of Boudicca

An anthology that encapsulates the Spirit of the defiant warrior in a modern apathetic age. No longer will the voices of our sisters go unheard, as the ancient Goddesses return to the battlements, calling to ignite the spark within each and every one of us—to defy oppression wherever we find it, and stand together in solidarity.

Warrior Queen: Answering the Call of The Morrigan

A powerful anthology about the Irish Celtic Goddess. Each contributor brings The Morrigan to life with unique stories that invite readers to partake and inspire them to pen their own. Included are essays, poems, stories, chants, rituals, and art from dozens of story-tellers and artists from around the world, illustrating and recounting the many ways this powerful Goddess of war, death, and prophecy has changed their lives.

Re-visioning Medusa: from Monster to Divine Wisdom

A remarkable collection of essays, poems, and art by scholars who have researched Her, artists who have envisioned Her, and women who have known Her in their personal story. All have spoken with Her and share something of their communion in this anthology.

Original Resistance: Reclaiming Lilith, Reclaiming Ourselves

Through poetry, prose, incantation, prayer and imagery, women from all walks of life invite you to join them in the revolutionary act of claiming their place—of reclaiming themselves.

On the Wings of Isis: Reclaiming the Sovereignty of Auset
For centuries, women have lived, fought and died for their equality, independence and sovereignty. Originally known as Auset, the Egyptian Goddess Isis reveals such a path. Unfurl your wings and join an array of strong women who have embodied the Goddess of Ten Thousand Names to celebrate their authentic selves.

Inanna's Ascent: Reclaiming Female Power
Inanna's Ascent examines how females can rise from the underworld and reclaim their power, sovereignly expressed through poetry, prose and visual art. All contributors are extraordinary women in their own right, who have been through some difficult life lessons—and are brave enough to share their stories.

New Love: a reprogramming toolbox for undoing the knots
A powerful combination of emotional/spiritual techniques, art and inspiring words for women who wish to move away from patriarchal thought. *New Love* includes a mixture of compelling thoughts and suggestions for each day, along with a "toolbox" to help you change the parts of your life you want to heal.

Hearts Aren't Made of Glass
My Journey from Princess of Nothing to Goddess of My Own Damned Life—by Trista Hendren.

How to Live Well Despite Capitalist Patriarchy
This book will serve as a starting point to challenge some of our societal assumptions, in hopes of helping women become stronger and breaking their chains.

The Girl God
A book for children young and old, celebrating the Divine Female by Trista Hendren. Magically illustrated by Elisabeth Slettnes with quotes from various faith traditions and feminist thinkers.

My Name is Medusa
The story of the greatly misunderstood Medusa, including why she likes snakes. *My Name is Medusa* explores the "scary" dark side, the potency of nature and the importance of dreams. Arna Baartz gorgeously illustrates this tale by Glenys Livingstone, teaching children (big and small) that our power often lies in what we have been taught to fear and revile.

www.thegirlgod.com

Table of Contents

Introduction

Mentorship with Goddess: Growing Sacred Womanhood

This book has been a long-time gestating. It is the book I wish my mother had been given to read, digest, and parent with. It is the book I wish had been available for me just before I started my periods. It is the textbook I wish I had been taught from at school. It is also the book I wish I had been able to access before giving birth to my daughter or failing that, had been able to read prior to her starting her periods. Finally, more recently, it is the workbook I wish I had completed before perimenopause began.

Unfortunately, none of this happened. The book did not exist.

Instead, it has been birthed through me and my life journey.

I was born with the seed of longing for Mentorship with Goddess. I knew in my body I wanted to be a Sacred Woman. I started searching for her in the Anglican Church and Christian Theology. I loved Mary, but the way she was painted and portrayed was disempowering. I really did not want to be an eternal virgin or, when the time came, a self-sacrificing mother. Mary Magdalene fascinated me – I fantasised she was Jesus' lover long before that entered mainstream forums. However, I was terrified I had the seven demons in me too, a fear which I kept hidden through concern I would be labelled a whore, or insane. At school and then university, I hunted for Goddess in the curriculum and asked my teachers and lecturers. There was nothing to be learned and they were deafeningly silent.

I started teaching and saw first-hand that my own adolescent challenges and longings were being universally repeated. The need for mentorship with Goddess and how to grow into a sacred woman was still needed well beyond the 1980s. Young women continued to struggle year after year, decade after decade, with the same issues – how to be well, how to be compassionate and loving towards themselves, how to self-care, how to end generational dysfunction, how to unravel and extricate themselves from patriarchal conditioning, how to self-lead, how to feel sovereign, and how to move from Princess to Queen, from child to woman. Primarily, *how to know who they are* and *how to flourish*.

In feeling driven to address and change this, initially I thought of doing an academic research project on the topic of teenage girls' well-being and wrote a PhD proposal and considered submitting it. But it felt wrong and too constricting. I felt it would not create practical change.

Childrearing became my focus for a while – I gave birth to two sons and a daughter. It was my daughter's birth which impacted me most. I realised how ill-equipped I was at nurturing and growing the feminine. The knowledge and gnosis were absent within me. I made, and continue to make, many mistakes.

Time moved on and I progressed into perimenopause. Feelings accelerated. There was urgency. The need to *learn* and *experience* moved from a *longing* to a *must*. I had a second chance, a second adolescence. I had a final opportunity to *give birth to me* and hopefully support other women to do the same. It felt like it was now or never to seek Goddess, to know her intimately, embody her, and activate gnosis. To be true to myself.

And this is what I did. I started from scratch. I moved from mind to body, to soul, to Goddess, and back to body. I studied. I read. I listened. I felt, experienced, and synthesised all I had lived through, creating this workbook, a curriculum and programme, and mentorship with Goddess – Growing Sacred Womanhood.

This workbook is a rite of passage, for all women from the onset of puberty upwards. I feel it may be especially supportive for woman navigating perimenopause. It is also recommended for facilitators and teachers who work with teenagers and perimenopausal women, as well as Mothers, Grandmothers, Aunts, and older Sisters. It may serve Mothers and Daughters to work through the programme together, as a supportive, sharing, and bonding process.

My hope is that it serves the highest good of all, through the reclamation of the Feminine.

May it serve you personally and deeply. Thank you for joining me on this powerful journey.

Kay Louise Aldred

Welcome

Welcome to your Mentorship with Goddess Workbook.

As Goddess mentors you through this programme, you join the Sacred Women of this generation who are reclaiming the Priestess path.

A Sacred Woman is the embodiment of the Sacred Feminine. She already exists within you, waiting patiently for you to remember that. She is in your DNA. Indeed, you are her. A unique frequency and imprint of her, essential for the completion and wholeness of the collective feminine. Your body is the gateway to recalling this truth and this year's journey is principally about discovering, accepting, and loving yourself – and then simultaneously protecting and vulnerably showing your whole self in the world.

The world needs women to know themselves and live authentically. That was the guidance I received on why I had to write the book to facilitate this. And as my own calling is to education, evolution, and embodiment, it all synchronises and aligns. I am grateful to be of service to the collective humanity, to all women and the Feminine in this way.

What being the embodiment of the Sacred Feminine means for you will become clear as you learn and evolve through the mentorship that Goddess offers. No one can tell you; you must discover it for yourself. Self-leadership, self-management, and self-direction via internal wisdom, courage, and truth are the gifts of Goddess.

It's all within you.

Map of the Journey for the Northern Hemisphere

Mentorship with Goddess: Growing Sacred Womanhood

ule

Map of the Journey for the Southern Hemisphere

Mentorship with Goddess: Growing Sacred Womanhood

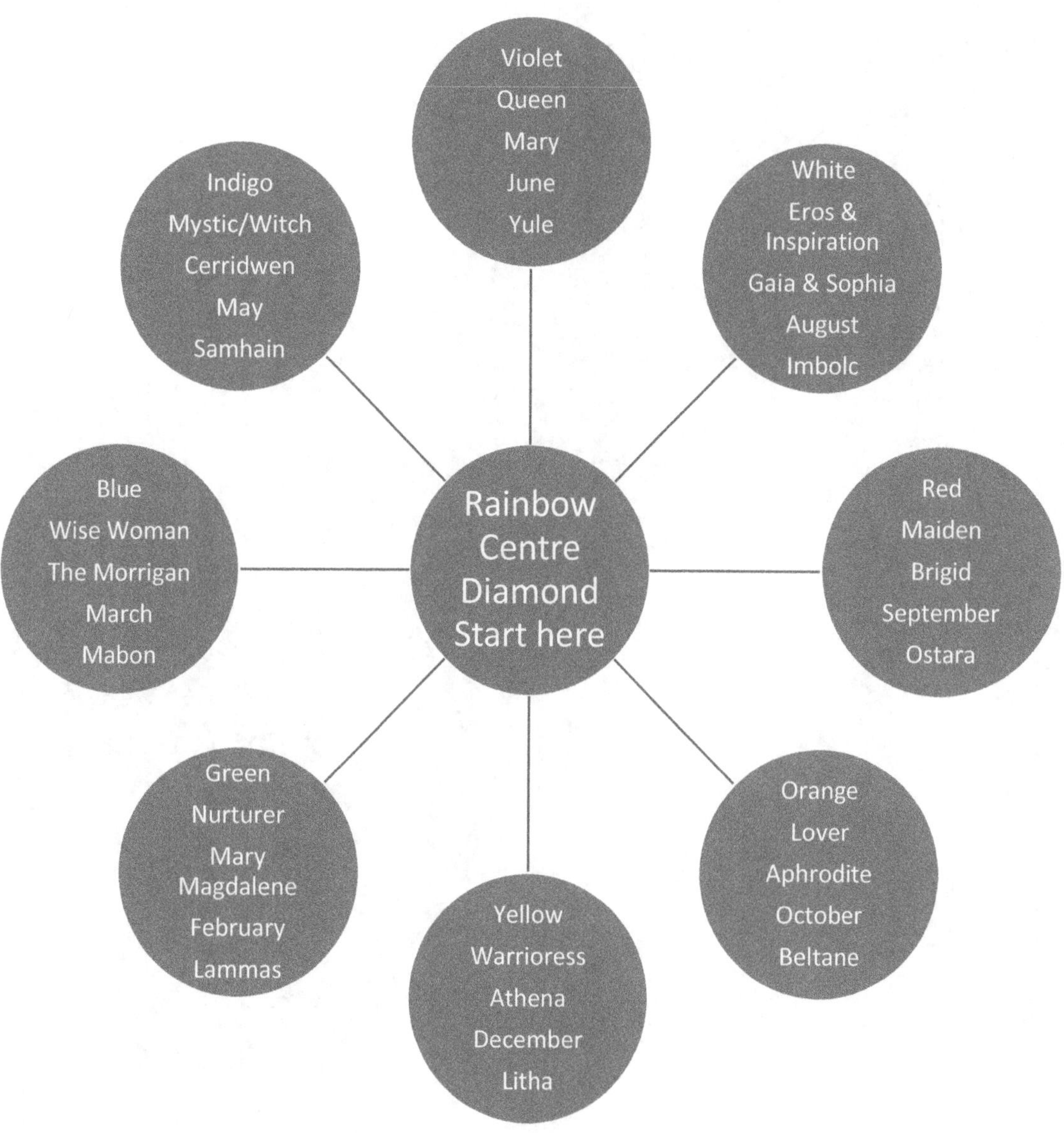

Painting by Kat Shaw

How to Use this Workbook

Having now seen a visual representation of the Sacred Womanhood Programme (see Map of the Journey) you are aware that the curriculum is split into 9 modules. The starting point being Rainbow Centre Diamond, followed by: February – White, March – Red, May – Orange, June – Yellow, August – Green, Sept – Blue, Oct – Indigo and Dec – Violet. Each module is broken down into smaller content and follows a similar format and structure to create regularity and predictability, supporting your mind to feel safe and know what to expect, so it can 'stand down' from analysing, strategising, and overthinking, making space for your body and heart wisdom to be felt, seen, and heard.

You can start the workbook at any point during the year, just remember to do the Rainbow Centre Diamond module first. Then do one module on the month as it is scheduled. Once you have completed all the modules, do the Initiation and Dedication Ceremony which is at the end of the workbook. Sometimes there is more than a month's gap between modules. There is a reason for this, the main one being time for absorption and integration. Try not to race ahead.

Each module, apart from the Rainbow Centre Diamond, is themed as a single colour and has a season, festival, moon cycle, animal, symbol, crystal, oil, body area, chakra, and Goddess archetype associated with it. These aspects of the mentorship and individually contain lessons and medicine for you.

There is a lot of information packed into each module which is why it is a good idea to slowly work through the content and activities throughout the entire month. It is not essential to *do* the whole of the module. It may be that working with the animal, for example, is enough. It may be that you return to the book several times over a few years. You cannot get anything wrong. You cannot make a mistake. This is a different type of education. It is self-discovery – one that is led by your body and capacity, not your mind.

When you begin the first module, you will already have prepared a tool kit in advance (see Before You Start). You can work through the book on your own, with a friend, or in a group. If you are working in a group, regardless of whether you have a nominated facilitator, please read the Notes for Groups and Facilitators page. As a group, ask questions, have fun, and listen to each other. Someone else might share something about Goddess which assists you to remember and reclaim.

If things get to be too much, it's ok to take time out. Stop. Rest. Do something different. See friends. Listen to music. Less is more. Then *always* start again. The deeper your commitment, self-reflection, and enquiry, the more you will grow into the truth of who you are.

Finally, please note that none of the information presented in this book is meant to replace the advice of a medical, health, legal and/or any other professional or service. How you choose to act on the words and content is of your own determination and free will.

This is the point of the mentorship; you assume the place as expert of yourself, knowing what is best for you; actions to take, how to be, what to eat, what to read, how to create, when to rest, who and when to ask for help and support.

These are the hallmarks of a Sacred Woman.

Note for Groups and Facilitators

Sitting in the circle of sacred sisterhood is subversive to the status quo. Extracting sisterhood from the patriarchal grasp of jealousy, gossip, put-downs, and competition is a political and revolutionary act. Facilitators are powerful role models and avatars of the archetype of Queen, demonstrators of self-sovereignty, self-leadership, and agency. They embody Goddess Mother, holding space, offering healthy attachment as the group learns to (re)parent themselves. Facilitators create a safe container for sharing and craft a space for

personal and collective courage and evolution.

As a group, meeting twice a month when a module is offered, is recommended.

Alternatively, facilitators could run the full programme as a two-week intensive.

Safety is paramount when women assemble and the group needs to agree upon a code, set of boundaries, and structure to allow for honesty, authenticity, and vulnerability. In addition, understanding the nervous system is vital for trauma-informed facilitation. The Rainbow Diamond Centre curriculum covers the nervous system in detail. Please read this in advance of the group's first session. Honouring group and individual nervous system capacity are vital for embodied, felt-sense safety.

The creation of a *Sacred Womanhood Code of Conduct and Commitments* can be done during the first session with participants. Here are some ideas of what to include:

- Self-responsibility
- Asking for support
- Honesty in sharing
- Confidentiality (and when things may need to be shared for safeguarding reasons, e.g., when there is a risk to self and others)
- Celebration and acceptance of difference
- Support for and commendation of authenticity
- Only offering advice if it is invited – allowing women to meet their own needs
- Respect for self and others
- Commitment to transformation
- Relationships as a learning opportunity
- Enjoyment
- Love

- Presence

- Sacredness of the Circle

- Commitment to listening and non-judgement

- Empowering self and others

- Privacy

- Joy and Play

- Magic

It might also be useful to create a group motto, slogan, or mantra. Here is an example which includes a mnemonic.

"I'm growing as a Queen in…

Self-responsible

Authentic

Courageous

Respectful

Empowered

Devoted

Womanhood."

Finally, think about logistics – where you will meet, the date and times, and the group size. Be clear from the start about these elements and adapt to the needs of the group if you can. Also, as a facilitator, it's important to set boundaries around contact outside of the session.

You can find an online evergreen 'Experience to Facilitate' course based on this workbook at https://thegirlgod.com/mentorship_with_goddess_course.php.

Before You Start

Prepare

You are about to embark on a journey of discovery. You will be exploring your entire body, mind, and energy. Commit to this fully. Place your hand on your heart now and pledge to unearth your Sacred Womanhood. Then prepare your Tool Kit.

Tool Kit

Make sure you have your own copy of this workbook. Write your name on it. Get used to the idea of it being a living document. The workbook is simply a skeleton – your words, experiences, and remembrances are the living flesh.

In addition, find a new notebook to journal and draw in throughout the year. Purchase some new pens to write with, the colours of each module ideally, white (pale pink or light grey is a good alternative), red, orange, yellow, green, blue, indigo, and violet. Any shade is fine. Plus, buy a special pen for the first rainbow diamond. Choose one that you are drawn to or select a favourite.

Other items you need:

- A large piece of cloth – any colour or design. You choose.
- A shell.
- A stone or crystal for each module – white, red, orange, yellow, green, blue, indigo, violet. Suggested crystals for each module include clear quartz, red jasper, carnelian, citrine, rose quartz, lapis lazuli, fluorite, and amethyst. These can be raw or polished, big, or small.
- Candles and matches.
- Sage bundles or Palo Santo sticks to energetically smudge/cleanse rooms and spaces.

You can find a Tool Kit for this workbook at http://thegirlgod.com/mentorship_toolkit.php.

There is also a Mentorship with Goddess Private Facebook Group for those who wish to be in community: https://www.facebook.com/groups/mentorshipwithgoddess.

REMEMBER THIS IS A YEAR OF GROWTH

You will get out of this year what you give. All that is really needed from you is your time, commitment, and desire to expand. You cannot do or get anything 'wrong.' Your truth and inner knowing, your wisdom, heart, and longing are never mistaken. That is the primary realisation.

Dedication:

All for my daughter *Elizabeth*.

This is the book I wish I had been able to write for you before you were born.

I love you.

Introduction to the Rainbow Centre Diamond Module

KEY CONCEPTS TO INTEGRATE:

- CHOICE: There are always a variety of options to choose from.
- FLOW: Moving with the constant change that is life.
- MENTORSHIP: Guidance you receive from Goddess, the Feminine.
- GNOSIS: Your inner knowing. Knowledge of Goddess, The Feminine, within you.
- SELF: Your unique identity.

Let us formally begin.

The Rainbow Centre Diamond enrols you into your Mentorship with Goddess as you begin to uncover your *gnosis* and retrieve the mysteries of the Feminine from *within* you.

We live in such a head-led, externally knowledge-based society and are used to being educated from books and a teacher. The majority of Goddess and Feminine Wisdom has been suppressed and eradicated from our consciousness, *his*tory, and schooling. For these reasons, this first module offers you a lot of intellectual material with the aim of you filling in any gaps in your knowledge and awareness so you can journey deeper into the Feminine.

The intention of this module is to restore her-story and activate rapid growth within you. The content will offer the missing pieces to the jigsaw puzzle of living in a woman's body, which once completed, helps you to break free from patriarchy.

I define patriarchy as dominance of 'the masculine' – mind, logic, and rational thinking, to the exclusion of 'the feminine' – body and earth, intuition, and instinct. In addition, patriarchy, for me, is the use of woman as a resource for another's gain and the suppression of creativity.

There is collective power offered to us from the circle of Goddess archetypes individually explored within each module. They are offered as archetypical guides of the Sacred Feminine. The Rainbow Diamond Centre module is inviting you to feel and know that these Goddesses are already present *within* you. They *are* you and you have the *choice* to activate their power and receive assistance from any one of them, at any time. Faith in this accelerates a deepening trust in *flow*, as you are reminded that your unique *self* – at the core of the diamond – is protected and safe to *shine*. You are the rainbow. Knowledge is power and there is nothing more powerful than knowing your*self*.

The Rainbow Diamond Centre *expands* your mind, body, and energy – and opens the doorway to Queendom and your crowing in Self-Sovereignty, Self-Leadership and Self-Parenting.

If you would like more support to guide you through this first module, you can purchase The Rainbow Diamond Centre Module Workshop at thegirlgod.com/the_diamond_centre.php.

Essential Understanding of the Nervous System

Understanding stress and the nervous system – its functions, trauma, and stress responses – is vital for Sacred Womanhood. This knowledge can reduce any fear we have in relation to our own body, particularly its sensations and reactivity. It's only when we can recognise that our bodies are doing their 'job' and trying to keep us safe, that we begin to trust them and have a willingness to foster a relationship with them. Once we appreciate and accept our moment-to-moment 'capacity' and tend to our bodily needs, choosing to self-soothe and self-care, we start to see positive outcomes in health and cultivate a deep connection with the wisdom held within our body's messages.

When we anchor into embodiment, we incarnate, and we feel safer to be our authentic self in the world.

Embodiment is the foundation of Sacred Womanhood, as body is Goddess. We can partner with our body, once we feel safe within it, to create magic and to manifest. The key areas of embodied magic are our womb space, heart space, and mind space. More about this later.

So, what is the nervous system?

On the following page is a basic diagram based on Stephen Porges' Polyvagal Theory of the nervous system. It shows the different parts of the nervous system.

At the base of the model is the ventral vagal portion, the social engagement and parasympathetic aspect of the nervous system. This is the place of safety where we feel connected to others and our environment and are present in the here and now. We are curious, rest and digest and our immune system works well. Humans are meant to operate from this part of the nervous system most of the time.

The middle section of the diagram is the sympathetic portion, the fight and flight area, activated in response to stress or a perceived threat. We need some sympathetic energy in our nervous system to support action and thinking. However, if we spend too long in activation, we start to experience an escalation of emotions and body symptoms. These include anxiety, and panic – known as flight – where we move away from the threat and anger and rage – known as fight – where we move towards the threat aggressively. Sympathetic activation increases blood pressure, heartbeat, and adrenaline – pupils dilate, we feel sweaty, and digestion and immunity slow down. Plus, we feel less connected to others.

Finally, if we feel we cannot escape stress or the threat, we move into freeze, the dorsal vagal portion of the nervous system. Here the body immobilises and collapses. We are completely overwhelmed, feel helpless, numb, depressed, and can dissociate. In freeze we also 'shut down.' There is a decrease in heartbeat, blood pressure, body temperature, eye contact, immunity, and social connection. We experience shame and feelings of entrapment, and the body prepares for 'death.' There is one other way the nervous system responds to stress and trauma and that is called fawn/fit in. This people-pleasing response is common in women and is a mixed state of fight/flight and freeze.

The action of the nervous system is incremental, so when stressed or activated we can flow up from social engagement through flight, fight, to freeze and then back down through fight and flight (deactivating) to social engagement. In extreme threat, or in response to a stressor which feels life threatening due to a previous experience (a trauma response), we can go from ventral vagal (social engagement) to dorsal vagal (freeze) immediately. In coming out of freeze we do however always move through the flight and fight deactivation.

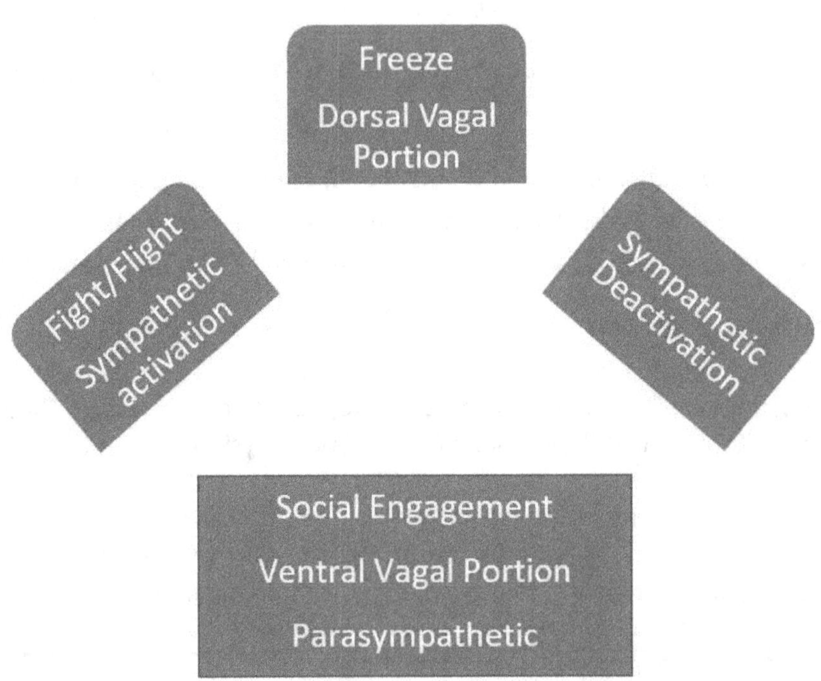

__What is stress?__

A stressor is the trigger for the activation of the body's (the nervous system sympathetic portion) stress response. The aim is to recognise the activation and your body's preferred way of responding – whether it be flight, fight, fawn, or freeze and to stay present to it, taking steps to both manage and reduce it, using the mind and body techniques.

What is your body's preferred stress response or responses?

Knowing and tending to your preferred stress reactions is self-care. Most of us have a combination of ways we respond and can find that we have different reactions with different people or situations.

Are you a fighter? Do you have an explosive temper? Are you bullying, controlling, entitled, perfectionist when stressed?

Are you a flighter? Do you experience obsessive and compulsive behaviours, anxiety, and perfectionism? Are you constantly doing and moving, worrying, and working?

Are you a fawner? Are you unable to express yourself and so are manipulated or controlled by others? Do you rarely use the word I? Are you a yes person, a people pleaser, tending, soothing, and caring constantly for others, without standing up for your own views, needs, and preferences?

Are you a freezer? Do you prefer hibernating instead of socialising and want to hide from reality? Do you experience spacey sensations, feel unreal, isolated, have brain fog, and find making decisions difficult?

So, what are your go-to responses? As you work through this programme, you will be given exercises to support your nervous system to regulate and bring you into the social engagement portion of the nervous system.

__What is trauma?__

Too much, too soon, too quickly.

Trauma is the reaction within the nervous system and brain, which occurs when someone does not have the capacity to stay present and digest an experience. The experience overwhelms the nervous system and takes it out of regulation. Trauma stays in our system, circulating and repeating until it is completed and integrated.

Understanding trauma, yourself, and working with trauma-informed facilitators, helps you to stay in your window of tolerance and regulation, so that you stay in safe in your body and not become overwhelmed, traumatised, or retraumatised further. Our trauma responses tend to follow the same pattern as our stress responses.

If you know you have trauma in your system that is being replayed in your life, it may be useful for you to work with a trauma specialist or practitioner. To learn more about all this look at the work of Irene Lyon. Her website is listed in *Further Exploration: A Growing Sacred Womanhood Resource List* at the end of the workbook.

What can you do to support nervous system regulation, and make your body become more resilient to stress and expand your capacity?

Firstly, recognising your capacity and taking self-responsibility to pace and live according to it, is vital. Working within the boundaries of our nervous system, titrating experiences, and information, knowing 'less is more,' and allowing for digestion and integration of content and sensation, is how we expand and empower our body wisdom. Expanding capacity comes from being able to slow down, track sensations, and to listen and respond to our body's messages about people and situations. More about how to do this in later modules.

The Basics

Do this practice several times a day.

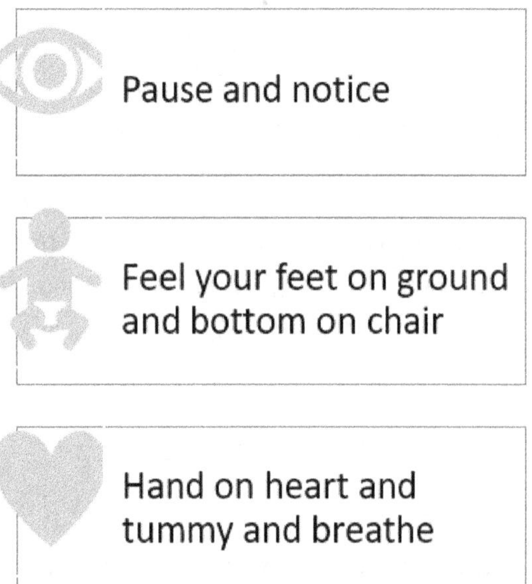

The SOS

This SOS exercise is designed to bring the body, mind, and nervous system into containment and a more manageable state.

The photo shows you how to do the practise – the right hand goes under the left armpit and the left hand around the top of the right arm. It seems so simple and yet its self-soothing and regulating effects are powerful since the activity allows the body to feel held, witnessed, and contained. If you can say kind words to yourself at the same time, such as, 'may I be safe' or 'you are held,' it is even more impactful.

Building Capacity

Committing to this embodied mindfulness technique will also expand your nervous system capacity. Whenever you feel a stress response in your body:

- Pause and feel it
- Notice the sensations in your body
- Listen to breath
- Feel feet on ground
- Bring your attention to your hands
- Notice your pelvis, legs, and feet
- Orient – look around your environment

The Maintenance

Self-holding exercises, when done daily, empty the body's stress pot. Placing your palms on various parts of your body – especially the womb, stomach, heart, forehead, back of head and nape – contains, regulates, and ensures the body feels listened to. These exercises can be done in bed to support sleep.

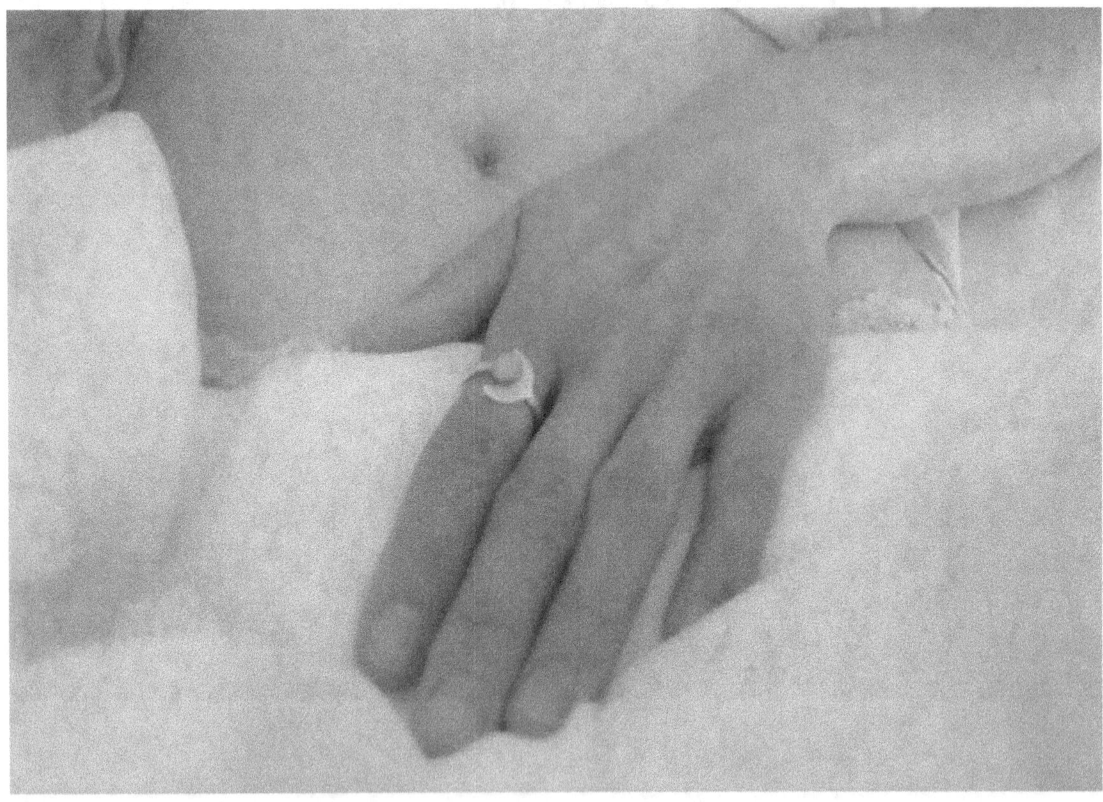

Breathing

Left Nostril Breathing creates calmness, emotional balance and lowers stress response.

- Sit comfortably
- Close your right nostril with your right thumb
- Breathe deeply in and out only through your left nostril
- Continue for three minutes

6, 6, 6 Breathing supports relaxation and calms anxieties.

- **Inhale:** Breath in for the count of 6
- **Hold:** Hold the breath for count of 6
- **Exhale:** Breathe out for the count of 6

Shaking it Off

Shaking off stress like other mammals do can help. At the end of your school or workday put on your favourite music track and shake and dance – jiggling and wobbling your whole body.

Know your Go-To Resources

Resources are things or techniques we use to bring more pleasure (which is the antidote to stress) and regulation to the body and nervous system. They are actions that encourage self-soothing. Which resources work for your nervous system is individual to you. Here are some examples for you to consider as a starting point:

- Titration – less is more. Go 'slow and steady.'
- Boundaries – follow your body's lead when setting them. This ensures you feel safe.
- Grounding techniques.
- Breathing techniques.
- Blankets.
- Essential oils.
- Warm bath.
- Orienting – looking around and noticing the entirety of your current environment – floor to ceiling, ground to sky – panorama, colours, objects, smells, everything.
- Tracking your body sensations and listening to what they are saying and responding.
- Self-touch – connecting to your skin and different parts of your body.

Supporting the Nervous System with the Mind

Mindfulness

Being in the here and now in an embodied way soothes, resources, and builds capacity in the nervous system. It is a simple practice of noticing and being curious about your thoughts, feelings, and body sensations, all whilst remaining connected to the world around you.

A Self-coaching Technique

This response to stress involves cognitively assessing your reactions to a threat, trigger, or stressor. You work through four approaches to see which helps reduce the stress. Two strategies are *external* – avoid and alter – and involve considering if you can change the situation. The other two strategies are *internal* – adapt and accept – and involve assessing if you can change your reaction.

Thinking about the stressor, consider if you can…

Avoid it.

- Control the situation.

- Avoid the person or situation activating you.

- Say no.

- Do less.

Alter it.

- Request others change their behaviour.

- Communicate your feelings and needs.

- Set boundaries and organise your tasks and time.

Adapt to it.

- Adjust your expectations.

- Practice thought stopping/distraction

- Assess the cost and benefits of the situation.

- Assess the long-term impact. Will it still matter in five years' time?

Accept it.

Whilst asking, *how can I support myself to move through this?*

- Talk.

- Release yourself from the situation/person. Give it or them no more of your energy.

- Self-compassion.

- Learn and set new boundaries going forward.

Wellness

We are *self*-incarnate, sacred flesh. Our body is the vessel and vehicle through which the Goddess is animated. So, understanding well-being is an essential part of your mentorship.

Sacred Women are well. They make wellness their top priority. Start reflecting on what you need to be and stay well.

Here is a **wellness model** for you to consider.

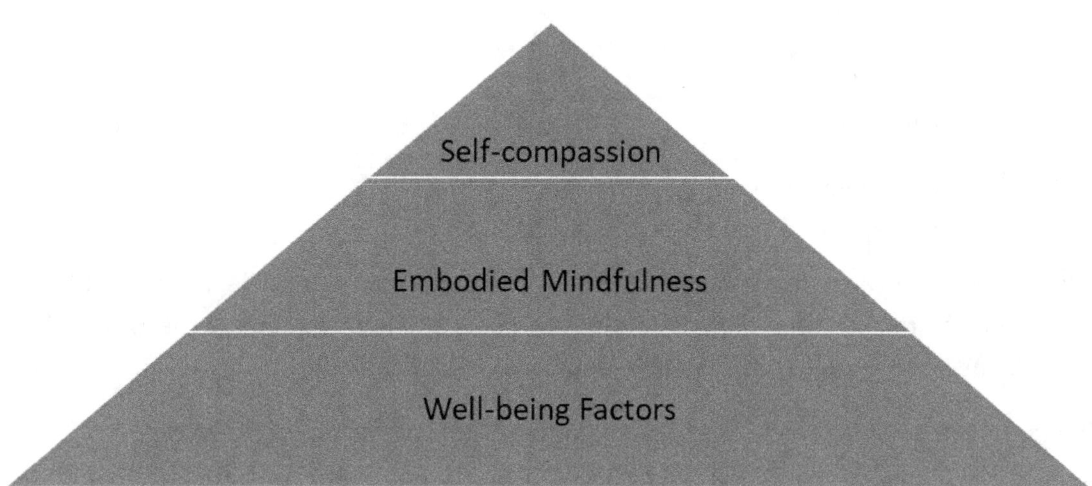

The base, the foundations of this wellness mode, are **factors which support well-being.** These include:

- Nutrition that suits and sustains you

- Hydration

- Movement

- Touch

- Sexual pleasure

- Functional breathing

- Restorative sleep

- Daylight

- Being in nature

- Health giving, toxin-free, physical environment

- Time out for self to recharge and decompress

- Tending to your nervous system

- Sense of identity

- Sense of meaning

- Emotional resilience

- Ability to ask for help

- Vulnerability

- Creativity

- Supportive, non-abusive relationships

- Social connection

- Being seen and heard

Once those factors are in place and working effectively for you, you will feel the benefit even more of a regular **embodied mindfulness** practice. Remember you are the expert of yourself and your body, so experiment with what works for you.

The top of this wellness model is **self-compassion**. This is the action of extending compassion to oneself in instances of perceived inadequacy, failure, or general suffering. It is being your own best friend and loving parent. Kristin Neff has defined self-compassion as being composed of three main components – self-kindness (not self-judgment), common humanity (not isolation), and mindfulness (not over-identification). There is a link to Kristen Neff's website in the *Further Exploration List* at the end of the workbook, but if you would like to experiment now with self-compassion, try this exercise below.

Self-Compassion Practise

Place your hands on your heart as you go to sleep and say these words to yourself several times:

May I be…

- Safe and peaceful

- Kind and accepting of myself

Energy

Sacred Women develop their own unique understanding of energy. This section of the workbook, however, may help you get started on this journey of discernment. The intention of the content below is for you to begin to navigate your path, feeling, sensing, processing, and working out the truth of energy for you.

What is Energy?

Everything is energy. Vibrating atoms. Frequency. Our bodies are energy, and they process energy. Energy moves through the body, passing through gateways, also known as chakras.

Energy wants to *flow*. It originates in the earth and cosmos. We also have the energy of our nervous system. Stagnation in the energy stream can cause dis-ease in us. Throughout the book you will explore this more deeply. The diagram on the next page will help you begin the process of visualising the flow of energy.

COSMIC Energy

Womb of Sophia

Wisdom

Inspiration (Air)

Light. Electric.

Upperworld

Hot, penetrating, action, SWORD

Enters the body via the SOUL STAR CHAKRA

THE BODY The Middle world

Crown

Third Eye

Throat

(all clockwise energy movement)

RECEIVE LOVE – Heart – GIVE LOVE

(all anti-clockwise energy movement)

Solar Plexus

Sacral

Root

Enters the body via the EARTH STAR CHAKRA

Cool, receptive, being, CHALICE

Underworld

Eros (Fire)

Lifeforce. Pulsating. Magnetic.

Creativity.

Womb of Gaia.

EARTH Energy

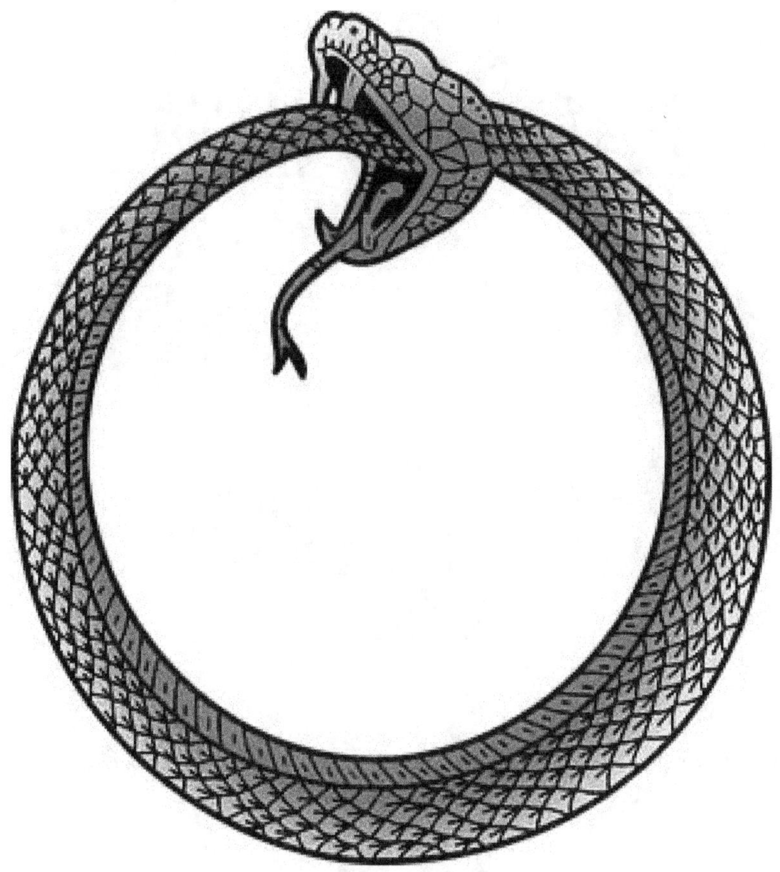

The Ouroboros – representing life-death-rebirth cycle.

Sacred Women understand cycles and live cyclically. They know that the cycles of their body are synced with those of the Earth and that they are one. Through continuous flow, movement, and change, women can rest, receive, vision, create and manifest. We will be exploring these concepts throughout the programme via the cycles listed on the following pages.

These are the cycles you will be learning about and working with.

The Directions

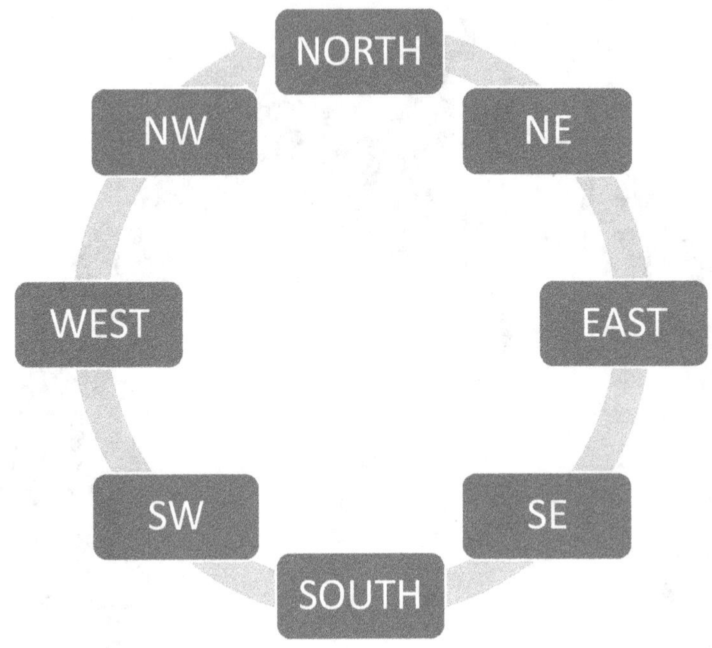

The Wheel of the Year

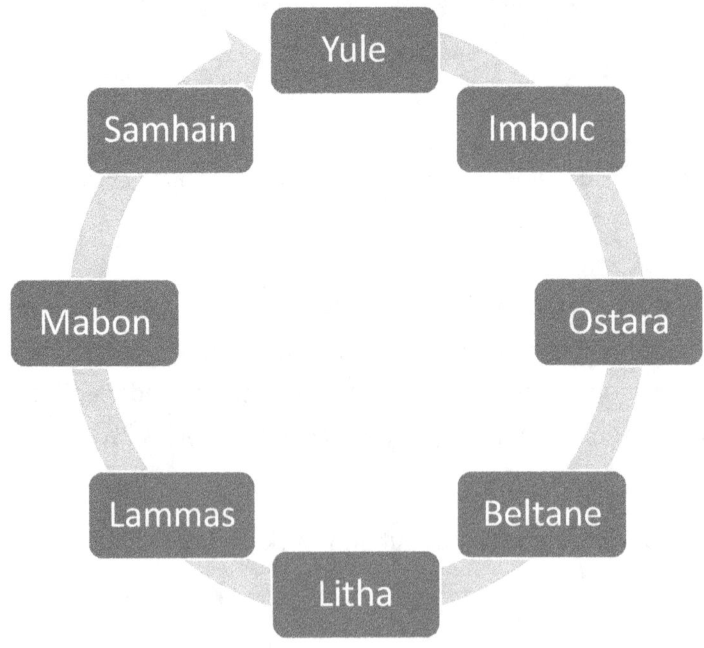

The Solstices and Equinoxes

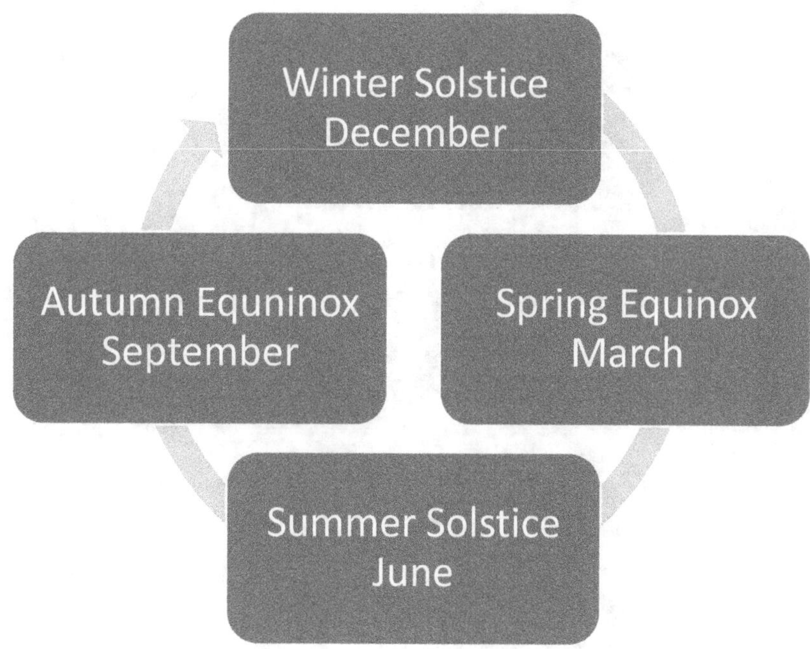

The Seasons

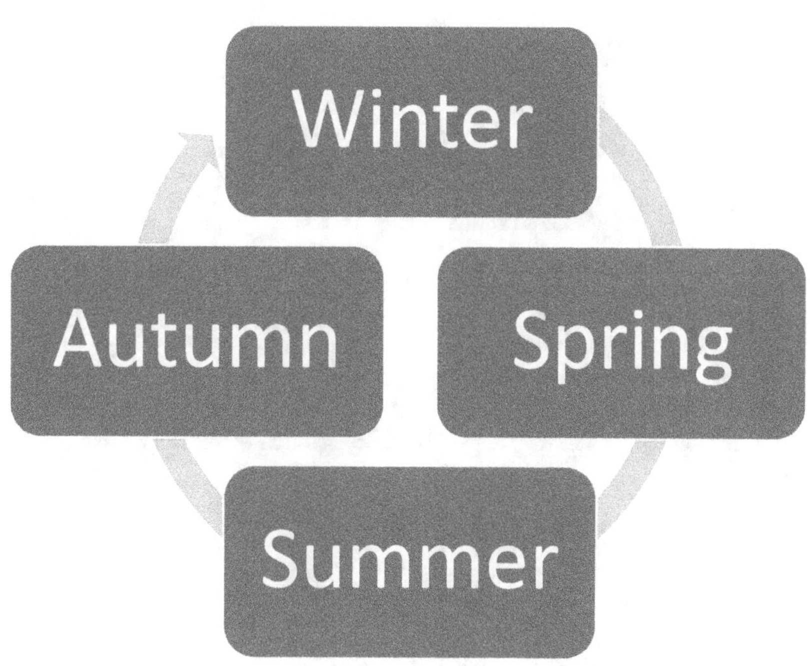

The Elements

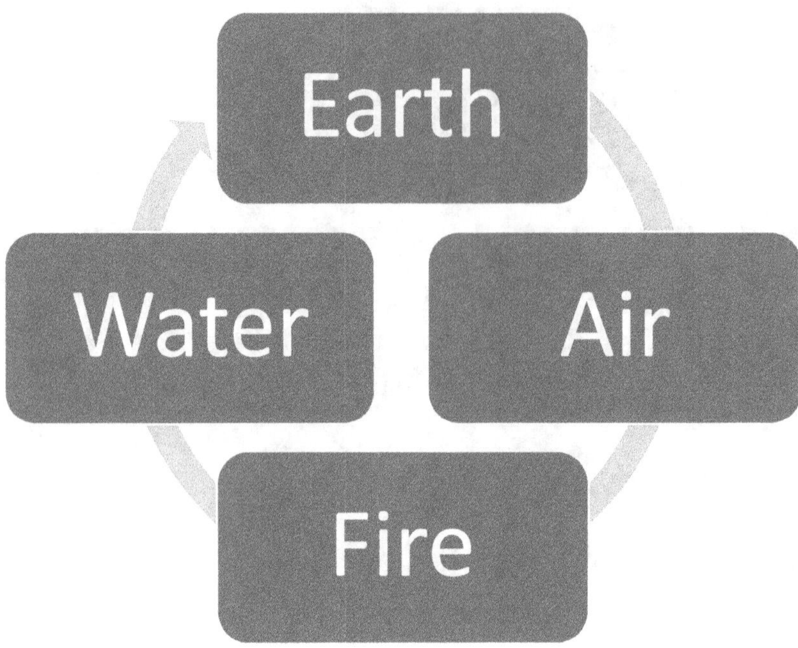

The Menstrual Cycle

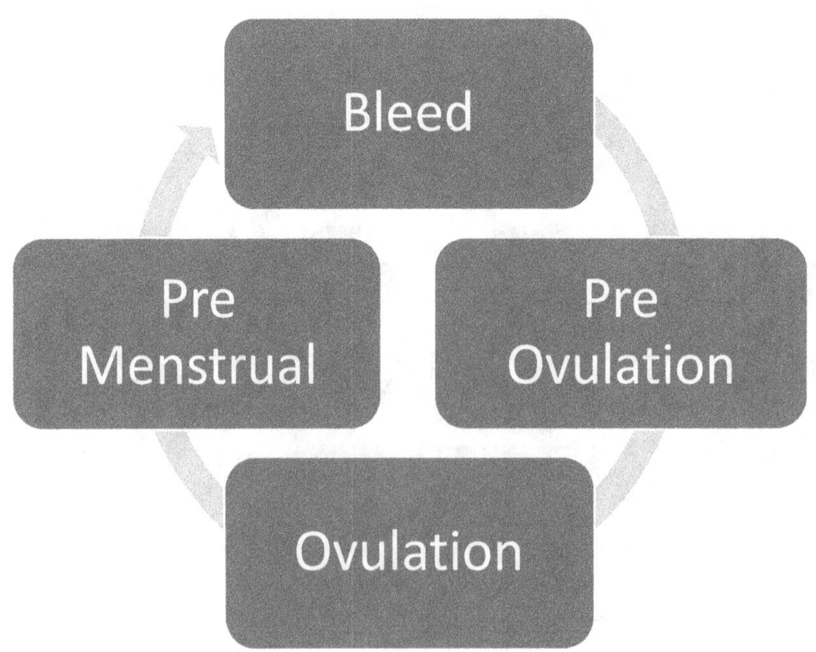

The Moon Phases

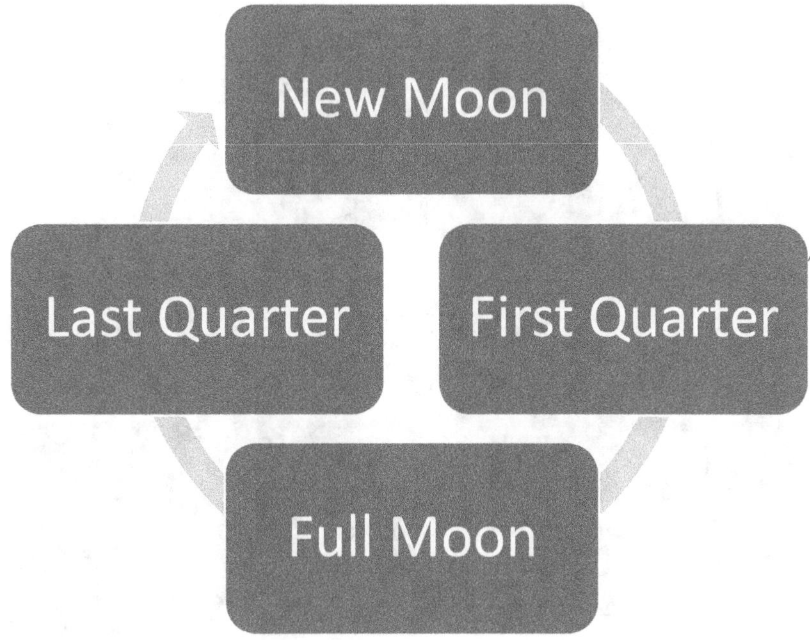

Energy Cycles

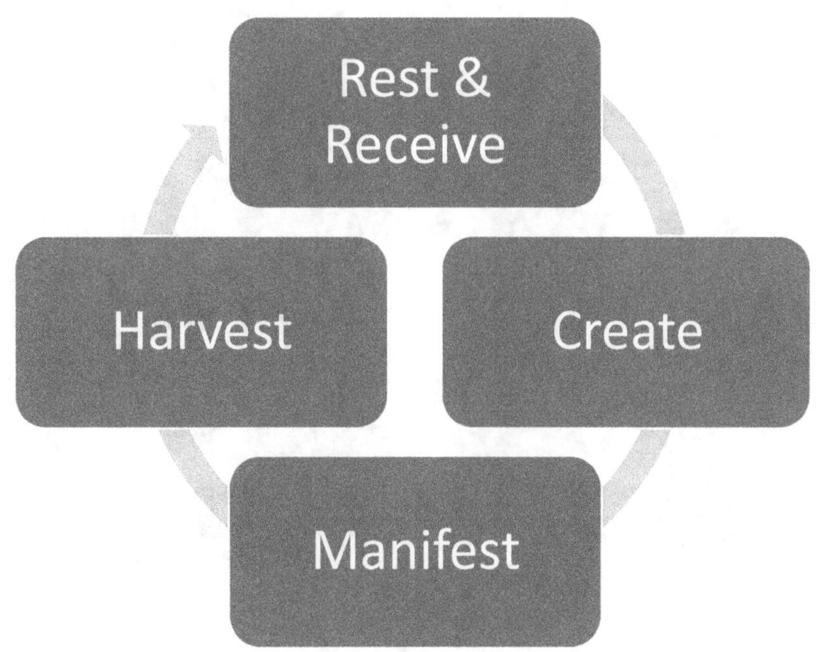

The Triple Goddess

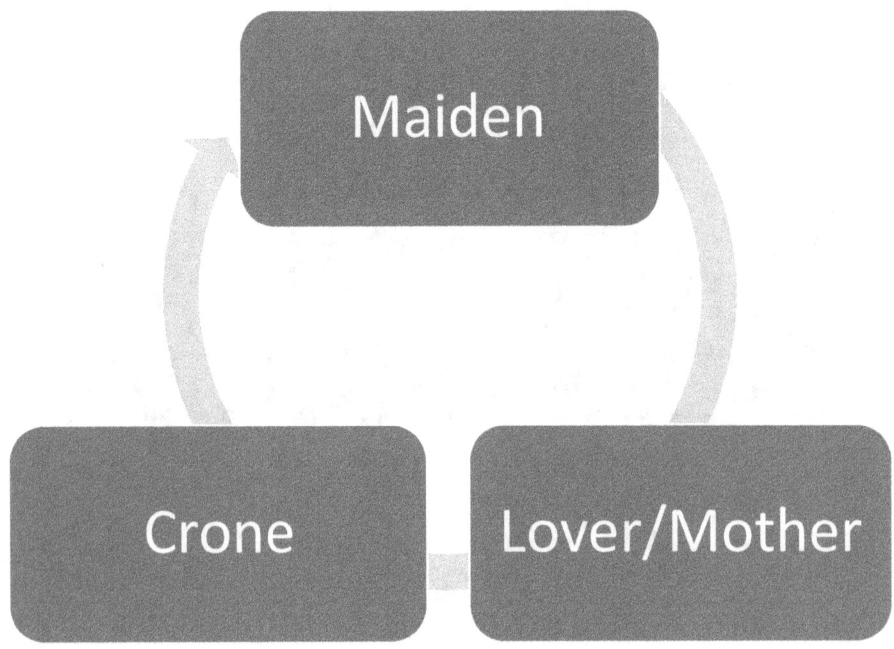
Maiden
Crone
Lover/Mother

Archetypes

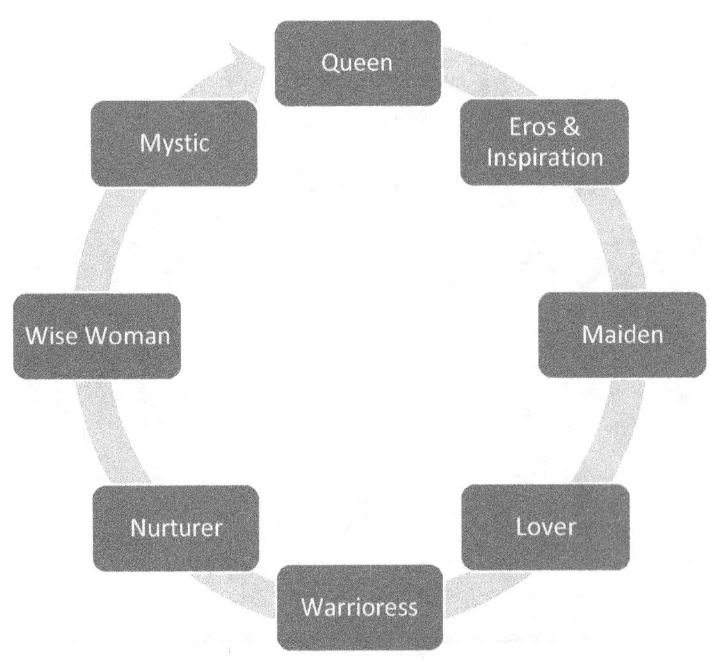
Queen
Eros & Inspiration
Mystic
Maiden
Wise Woman
Lover
Nurturer
Warrioress

Sacred Womanhood

Now is the time for you to start to explore and consider what Sacred Womanhood means for you.

Physically you are a fully developed woman by approximately 18 years. Your brain has fully developed around 24 years and by 28 years our 'Self' has matured and individuated. Your chakra system refines and matures throughout your lifespan.

Consider these questions:

- *When you think of a woman what comes to mind?*

- *What does the word Sacred mean for you?*

- *What is Sacred Womanhood for you?*

- *How would a Sacred Woman live, think, and act?*

- *What is Goddess for you?*

- *What is the Feminine for you?*

Your relationship to the Sacred Feminine will evolve and become bespoke to you. Defining it is a personal experience and decision, one which you will continually explore throughout the year. For some, the Sacred Feminine is an energy, for others a Goddess or Being. For others, it is a selection of qualities or gifts – such as creativity, nurturance, intuition, vision, sensuality, inclusion, and collaboration. Others see the Sacred Feminine as full embodiment. For many, it is a combination of all these things.

You will decide which it is for you.

This *Rainbow Diamond Centre* has taught you already that all the archetypes and aspects of Goddess are within you. They are frequencies and vibrations you can shapeshift into, amplify, and inhabit. During the year you will understand, feel, and know them intimately, activating the colours of the rainbow and the power of Goddess within the strands of your DNA, blood, bones, organs, body, mind, energy, actions, thoughts, and behaviours.

Right now, as you begin this year's journey, what is the Sacred Feminine for you?

You may not have answers for all the questions above. Some you may have no answer for, others only a few words to jot down. Wherever you are – with your thoughts and feelings around all these enquiries – is exactly where you need to be. Know that you can add to your answers as we go through the book. This is something to be encouraged. You can cross out what you originally thought and replace it with something new. Change is encouraged. Change is inevitable. Change is growth.

Code of Sacred Womanhood

Sacred Womanhood is bound by a code, a set of expectations, and commitments. If you are working through this programme in a circle of sisterhood, everyone needs to agree on what your code is and make a pledge of commitment to the sanctity of your circle and the journey you are undertaking together. For further information on this, see the *Note for Groups and Facilitators* section earlier in the workbook.

As an individual you also need to also make promises, pledges, and commitments to and for yourself. If you are working through this programme alone, the following exercise still needs to be completed.

Sacred Womanhood Code and Commitment

What do you want for Sisterhood?

What would you like to read in a Sisterhood Code of Conduct?

What are your top five intentions and commitments to this year of Mentorship with Goddess? Write them down here:

1.

2.

3.

4.

5.

Pledge

Put your hand on your heart and speak your five intentions and commitment aloud, knowing Goddess has heard you and that it is *all done*. You are complete.

If you would like additional support through the Diamond Centre Module, you can find a recorded course at http://thegirlgod.com/the_diamond_centre.php.

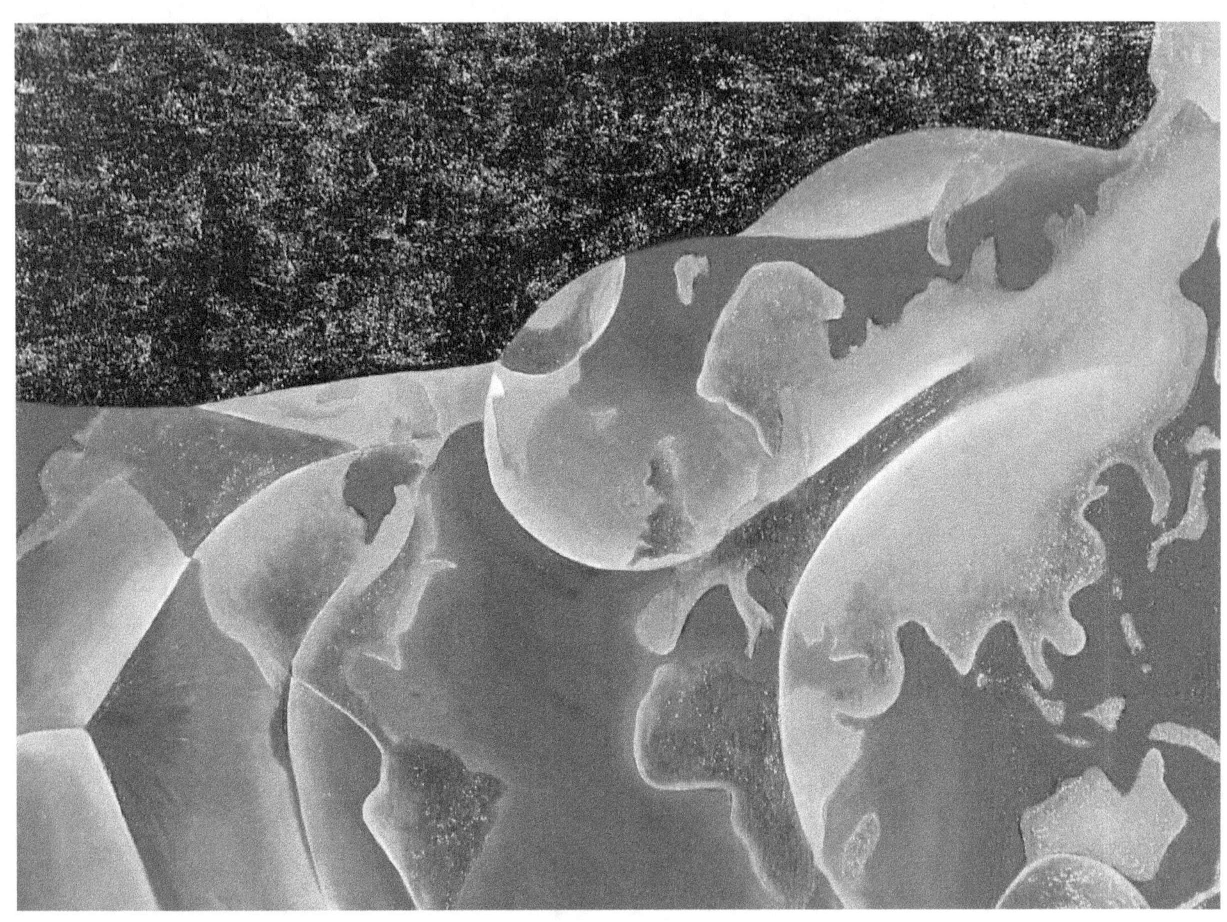

Painting by Kat Shaw

Introduction to White Module

KEY CONCEPTS TO INTEGRATE:

BOTH: Earth and Cosmos, Light and Dark, Human and Divine, Flesh and Energy. You are both.

ENTIRELY: You are everything – total, whole, complete. Your self is inseparable from Goddess.

BRIDGE: You are the channel and connector of Earth and Cosmic energy.

MIDDLE WORLD: Human realm.

LOWER or UNDER WORLD: The womb of Gaia (Goddess Mother Earth).

EROS: Force of aliveness, desire, instinct to live. Innate in everything. Active in our embodiment and imagination. Energy.

UPPER WORLD: The cosmos and womb of Sophia (Goddess Wisdom).

INSPIRATION: Creative spark. Energy.

CO-CREATRIX: Sacred Woman working in collaboration with Eros and Inspiration to create.

SOUL: Eternal LIGHT. Source origin. Energy.

Month: February

Season: Late Winter and Early Spring

Festival: Imbolc

Direction: North-East

Element: Earth

Goddess archetype: CO-CREATRX – Gaia & Sophia

Symbol: Star (five-point pentacle)

Animal: Dove

Moon: New Moon and Waxing Crescent

Menstrual: Menstruation

Body area: Nervous system. Soles of feet & palms of hands

Chakra: Earth Star and Soul Star

Crystal: Clear Quartz (healing, protection, transformation, amplification, activation)

Oil: Eucalyptus (mental clarity, invigorating, enhances meditation)

In this module, you will prepare, anchor into, and strengthen your body as the MIDDLE world, as BRIDGE between the LOWER and the UPPER WORLD (Earth and the Universe) – and stabilise your nervous system in preparation for receiving the energy flow of SOUL, EROS, and INSPIRATION.

Your DOVE – the energy offering the olive branch of inner peace which comes from living your truth of Sacred Womanhood – enables you to become a symbol and messenger of connection. Through your ability to anchor into the LOWER world, you share the energy of Gaia, Eros, passion, lifeforce, and desire. By flying high into the cosmos, the UPPER WORLD, you can embody more of Soul in the human realm, speaking, living, and acting from INSPIRATION and Sophia's wisdom. You activate the CO-CREATRIX frequency of Goddess.

Retrieving, bridging, and embodying these powerful energies requires your body and nervous system to be primed ready.

Everything with Goddess mentorship starts with the BODY. Self-care is essential for growing your Sacred Womanhood. It is entirely selfless as it sustains you as you sustain others, give from an overflowing cup of lifeforce, *and* it allows Goddess to take up more space on earth. The presence of the Feminine is essential on Earth and especially at this current time. Your nervous system needs to be as regulated as much as possible, so you can build capacity to channel and activate the rainbow Goddess frequencies within you. So that you EXPAND and become more of SELF and shine evermore brightly as SOUL.

CO-CREATRIX – *Goddesses Gaia and Sophia.* EROS and INSPIRATION

Gaia

The Greek Earth Goddess who has existed since the beginning of time. We walk on her body; our life is entirely reliant upon her. Our bodies receive sustenance and are provided for by her; elements and compounds needed to make shelter and clothes, to provide warmth, food, and water. Her womb, the lower world, catches and keeps safe the energies which split off from us during trauma until we are ready to retrieve them. Her electromagnetic field stabilises our nervous system. All life in the human realm is completely dependent upon this great Goddess.

Take a moment to reflect on this and your relationship with the Earth.

Sophia

In origin, Sophia is not a 'Goddess' but the primordial feminine creative energy, a cosmic force, which had existed since the beginning of time. Sophia is the Inspiration and Creatrix of everything. Wisdom in flesh is the Goddess Sophia. Some also believe that Sophia is the energy of Soul. She is the power of gnosis, inner knowing. As you get to know her 'face' and how she feels in your body, her qualities and gifts will become clear to you.

For now, consider these questions:

- *What do you understand as wisdom?*

- *Where did that understanding come from?*

- *If wisdom were a feeling in your body, where would it be?*

Keep coming back to them throughout the year, amending when you are moved to.

Welcome to February. The season of white. There is often snow this month as we move through the final stage of winter. We search for the first signs of Spring, the emergence of white snowdrops, and the signal of life returning after Gaia's inward retreat and descent into deep darkness of hibernation and slumber.

The festival of Imbolc falls on the Wheel of the Year halfway between the Winter Solstice, Yule and the Spring Equinox, Ostara. The calendared date for the festival is February 1st. At this festival we celebrate Gaia's reawakening and feel the vibration of her womb as lifeforce starts to gently pulsate from the Lower World. Simultaneously we also feel the first stirrings of Eros within us.

At this festival we ask our intuitive inner wisdom, Sophia within us, *what does lifeforce want me to create and express this year?*

In innocence and without expectation, our Dove receives messages, hunches, and instinctual hints of Inspiration that show us the path to take during the coming year. A lot of this will not be entirely new, as during the winter we have had a lot of time to vision and dream. The shift at Imbolc is that we start to *feel* the urges to act and co-create.

Light and candles are a huge part of this festival. They symbolise the catalysing of inspiration and creativity, the warming up and sparking of the nervous system into sympathetic action and the electricity of ignition of neural pathways as we start to design within the mind space. We can feel and receive this as we look at them. Simultaneously we feel the increasing heat of the womb space flame. Eros within us is starting to spiral and swirl – we are warming up in tandem with the Earth.

We need to reset our bodies, nervous system, and energy ready to receive flow.

Your Body, Nervous System, and Energy in February

February is a good time to reset, to 'cleanse,' regulate, and ground the body and the nervous system in preparation for the intense energies. It's time to anchor and build the bridge.

It's time to anchor into the earth and grow deep roots so you are stable and resilient enough to receive the strong energies which will flow through you from the earth and cosmos during the spring and summer months. Your body will now become a bridge between the earth and cosmos, so it is vital in February that you strengthen and fortify the structure and integrity of this.

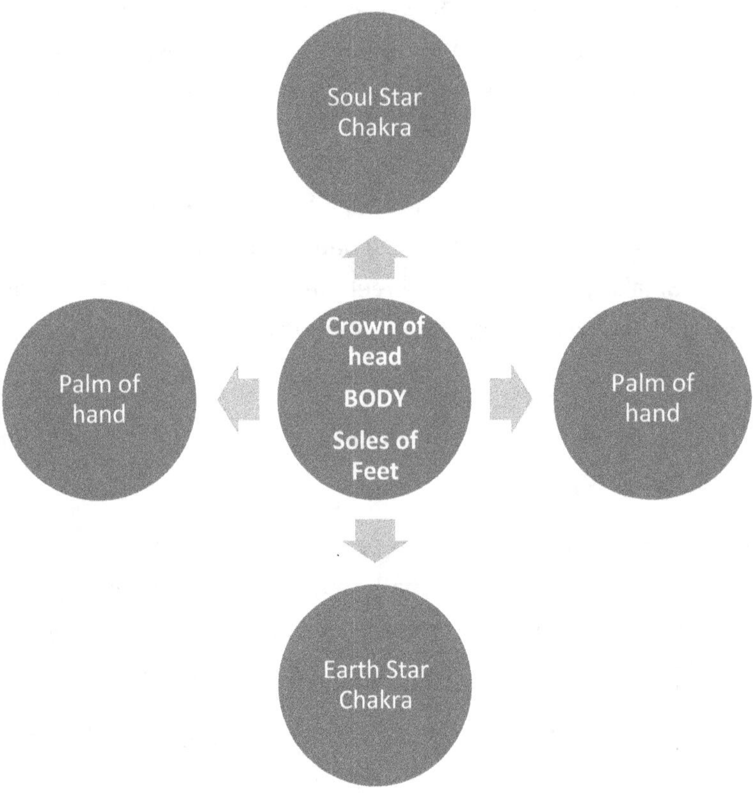

Kundalini energy is erotic energy – also known as lifeforce, serpent, or libido – which runs through the body. It is the double helix flow in our DNA and the spiralling energy of the nervous system from the base of the spine to the top at the nape of the neck. Eros flows from the womb of Gaia, through our earth star chakra (our brown super root located approximately 12 inches below the soles of our feet in the earth), through the soles of our feet into the perineum and up the spine and through the crown of the head, the soul star chakra (our halo, located a few inches above our head and up into the cosmos). Inspiration and the electric penetrating flash and sword of wisdom energy which moves from the cosmos, the womb of Sophia down through the soul star chakra, through the crown and down the spine, through the perineum, down and out through the souls of the feet, through the earth star chakra into the womb of Gaia. These are extraordinarily strong energies, and we need to prepare for the body and nervous system at Imbolc to receive them in advance of spring and summer, when they intensify.

How do we do that?

BODY

- Consider a light detox. Eliminate processed food. Eat whole foods, prepared, and cooked from scratch. As you do this assess your food relationship. Honestly appraise what nourishes and sustains you and feels good in your Goddess body temple.

- Drink less caffeine. Increase herbal teas, hot water, and lemon.

- Have warm Epsom salt baths. Use a salt scrub on your skin, moisturise with a light oil afterwards.

- Get outside. Start to increase sunlight and daylight on your eyes and skin.

- Move more. Introduce a daily 20-minute walk outside and gentle stretching in the morning.

- Start meeting up with people again. Increase social contact.

- Increase self-pleasure and sexual relationships when you feel the desire.

NERVOUS SYSTEM

- Do the containment and self-holding exercises from the Rainbow Diamond Centre Module.

MIND

- Vision, plan, and set intentions.

- Put Eucalyptus oil into an oil burner. This will start to open neural pathways and get your crown chakra ready for you to receive inspiration and wisdom seeds into your mind.

ENERGY

- Sage smudge your bedroom and bathroom. Open the windows, clear the energy.

- Prepare the womb space for Eros, conscious conception, and gestation of Inspiration and Light into form. Dance, moving the hips in a figure eight or sit cross-legged on a mat and create a spiral movement.

- Fill with Light. Take your hands to your soul star chakra, your halo. Place your palms onto the halo. Imagine your palms opening. Draw the Light of Soul, your halo light through the palms of your hands and feel it flow down the arms and into the heart. Imagine it mixing with your blood cells and then flowing around every part of your body.

- Clear the chakras. Take your hands to your soul star chakra, your halo. Place your palms onto the halo. Imagine the palms opening. Draw the Light of Soul, your halo light, through the palms of your hands – but this time make balls of Soul light in your hands. Take a ball of light to each chakra to clear and strengthen it. So, you take a ball of light to your root chakra (at the perineum), your sacral chakra (your womb space), your solar plexus (above the belly button but below the breasts), the heart space (centre of the chest), the throat, the third eye (the space at the centre of the eyebrows) and the crown (at the top of the head). There is a diagram on the chakra system in the Rainbow Diamond Centre module.

GROUND

Prepare and strengthen yourself as the BRIDGE of connection.

- Stand on the Earth barefoot if you can.

- Breathe into the soles of the feet and out into the earth three times. On the third exhale send a root from the soles of the feet through the earth star chakra and into Gaia's womb.

- Then place your palms flat onto the earth. Breathe into the palms of the hands and out into the earth three times. On the third exhale, send a root from the palms through the earth star chakra and into Gaia's womb.

- Stay breathing in and out with Gaia for three minutes each day in February.

- If it is cold, you can do this indoors.

Planting the Dream Seeds with a Crystal Grid and New Moon.

At the festival of Imbolc, we plant the big dream seeds we want to gestate throughout spring and bloom in summer. Setting intentions are vital, as a Sacred Woman *is* the magic, she is a Co-Creatrix, she merges her will with the will of Goddess. So, once we receive inspiration, we set the intention of what we want to manifest into form and then initiate the magic via a crystal grid.

Energy follows intention. Where our intention goes, energy flows. So, it is important to think carefully about the intention you want to set and check that the vision or dream you have *feels* good in your body.

Going forward throughout the year at every New Moon and menstrual bleed, we have the opportunity to set intentions to support the manifestation of bigger dreams. We also have a chance to check if those existing dreams still feel good, or if we have received other visions at Dark Moon (the two days before our menstrual bleed) which feel more aligned, if we want to change direction and intention set in relation to these instead.

As the moon becomes waxing crescent, the week after new moon, or days after we finish our menstrual bleed, we receive the connections, signs, and symbols from the universe as to how to take action to manifest the dreams.

Pentacle Crystal Grid and Magic Spell for Intention Setting and Manifestation

Crystal grids powerfully amplify intentions and manifestation. This amplification is stronger if the grid is placed on a sacred symbol. The sacred symbol of the Pentacle (also known as the witch's cross or pentagram) is an ancient totem of protection, life, blessings, and health. It also represents feminine gnosis and knowledge. Its powerful origin is within the apple core pentacle of Gaia. Cut an apple in half through the middle and see the sacred symbol in the centre for yourself.

What you need:

- A clear quartz crystal (ideally a crystal point)
- Five other smaller crystals or stones
- Pen
- Paper to trace out the Pentacle on the pages that follow
- Candle

- Sage stick for smudging
- Matches

The spell:

- Burn some sage to smudge and energetically clear the area you are doing the magic spell in.

- Make sure you will be undisturbed.

- Take three deep breaths. Make sure you are 'in' your body.

- Ground and root yourself into Gaia's womb.

- Place your hand on your womb and forehead and think about your vision, your dream seed.

- Then create three intentions of what you would like to birth into form that feel good to you. Remember to check in with your body and keep the intentions focused on sensation and feeling. For example, loving family relationships or inner peace.

- Write them on a piece of paper, fold it up, and place it in the centre of the star.

- Call forth Soul, the power of Goddess, Gaia, Sophia and the power of your womb, heart, and mind.

- Place the five stones at each point of the star.

- Hold your clear quartz in your hand and starting at the top point, hold the crystal over the point and say, 'By the power of the moon I am receiving… ' and say your three intentions out loud.

- Hold the clear quartz over the second point and say, 'By the power of my body I am receiving…' and say your three intentions aloud.

- Hold the clear quartz over the third point and say, 'By the power of Gaia I am receiving…' and say your three intentions aloud.

- Hold the clear quartz over the fourth point and say, 'By the power of Sophia I am receiving…' and say your three intentions aloud.

- Hold the clear quartz over the fifth point and say, 'By the power of Goddess I am receiving…' and say your three intentions aloud.

- Then place the clear quartz over the folded paper and say, 'It is done' three times, 'and so it is' three times, and then finish by saying, 'This is for the highest good of all.'

Speak clearly and confidently – you are 'spelling out' what you want.

Leave the grid in place for 2-4 weeks, depending how you feel and what manifests. Then take it apart in reverse order, stone by stone, with gratitude and thanks to the moon, your body, Gaia, Sophia, and Goddess.

Painting by Kat Shaw

Introduction to Red Module

KEY CONCEPTS TO INTEGRATE:

BALANCE: Equilibrium.

MAIDEN: Original essence. Whole. Complete.

BLUEPRINT: Origin.

EROTIC INNOCENCE: Free, shameless, unconditioned safety of lifeforce, power, and embodiment.

INNER CHILD: Aspect of self that is innocent and open and full of wonder, joy, awe, presence, and spontaneity.

GROUNDING: Connecting and anchoring into the electromagnetic charge and red energy of the earth.

EMBODIMENT: Incarnation, in flesh.

BREATHING: Inhale and exhale.

HYDRATION: Absorbing water.

GROWTH MINDSET: Enjoys discovery and learning. Considers the perspective of others. Resilience.

METACOGNITION: Thinking about thinking.

CURIOSITY: Inquisitiveness.

PLAY: Fun and enjoyment.

CREATIVITY: Moving and doing with inspiration and eros.

    Month: March

    Season: Spring

    Festival: Ostara

    Direction: East

    Element: Air

Goddess archetype: MAIDEN – Goddess Brigid

Symbol: Egg

Animal: Hare

Moon: First Quarter

Menstrual: Pre-Ovulation

Body area: Perineum, Anus and Base of the Spine

Chakra: Root

Crystal: Red Jasper (grounding, stability, strengthening circulation and fortifying the blood)

Oil: Cypress (grounding, energy, connection to nature)

In this module, you will connect with your MAIDEN, the most ancient aspect of Self, your original essence, that which is whole, unconditioned, and untamed, and which holds Soul BLUEPRINT, your origin, and the uniqueness of being. The frequency of your Maiden also holds your EROTIC INNOCENCE, the free, shameless, and unconditioned safety of your lifeforce, power and pleasure-full EMBODIMENT. She also gifts you your INNER CHILD, your wonderment, joy, awe, spontaneity, and pure presence. This part of you is one with nature and the spirit of aliveness. Through reconnection, CURIOSITY and CREATIVITY are activated, and you begin to PLAY again, prioritising fun, enjoyment, discovery, and learning. You embrace METACOGNITION and move from a fixed to a GROWTH MINDSET, excited to discover, see the world from a different perspective, adjusting the lens of your vision to one of inquisitiveness. Every challenge becomes an opportunity for growth. You see that there is no failure, and your resilience grows.

Bonding with nature is integral to this module. Through GROUNDING, you feel more connected, safe and know you belong. Your body feels safer as Gaia supports you to become more balanced and stabilised. Considering what you need for BALANCE is essential to this module. Assessing and making the necessary changes – so that the power of red, erotic lifeforce, and Gaia's energy can flow through you – is the heart of this module and month, as it creates fertile ground for your dreams and visions to grow and your creativity to flourish.

You ARE BREATHING nature in, especially the element of Air during spring. This revitalises and energises your mind, body, and energy, and supports balance. HYDRATION, ingesting the element of water, supports the body to come into equilibrium too, through detoxification. It moistens the womb space, cultivating fertile ground. Through breath, inspiration implants in the body and with the support of the Gaia's energy, gestates dream seeds and births them into form.

During this module you become conscious to how energy, soul, and Goddess fuse with matter, flesh, and humanness – galvanising your Sacred Womanhood incarnation.

MAIDEN – Goddess Brigid

Brigid, the Bright One, is an Irish Goddess of the dawn, fertility, and sacred wells. She is the Goddess of inspiration and healing and is often considered the patron of creatives, especially poets, medical professionals, and healers. In addition, she is often named the Triple Goddess of the Fires (of the home – the hearth, the smithy – the forge and inspiration – creativity). Brigid is the perfect archetype to connect with at Ostara and mentor for this month because she encapsulates all the elements and polarity into union within her – Goddess of inspiration (air), the smithy and hearth (fire), the well (water) and healing/the body (earth). Her flaming ginger hair, and her triple amplification of fire, connects her strongly with the RED of this module.

Brigid, Goddess of the smithy and hearth, of fire.

Brigid, Goddess of the well, of water.

Take a moment to reflect on this and your relationship with the polarity and unity. *How are you with paradox?*

Welcome to March. The season of Red. The Earth wakes up and so do we. Lifeforce starts to pulsate and flow, new life emerges. Suddenly spring has sprung. Our vitality returns. We have more energy. We move into a place of feeling a need to assess and create balance by changing habits, behaviours, and thoughts. Less of some, more of others.

The festival of Ostara, the Spring Equinox, falls on the Wheel of the Year halfway between Imbolc and Beltane. The calendared date for the festival is March 21st or 22nd. At this festival, day and night and dark and light, are of equal length. This time is all about the amalgamation and synthesis of polarity. Heaven and earth, inner and outer, body and spirit. There is a reclamation of our erotic innocence, our pure lifeforce, sensuality and primal connection with the RED Dragon bloodlines of Gaia – which gatekeeps, fiercely protects, and guards our Maiden from who all new life and creation comes – should we choose to lean into that offering. So, like the EGG we encapsulate our entire potency, our untainted lifeforce, within the protection of our skin shell which in turn is protected by the energy grid and Dragon energy of Gaia. Grounding into this strengthens us and creates safety for our innocence.

At this festival we shapeshift between the fire of embodiment and Eros and the airy consciousness of Inspiration, seeking balance and relationship between the two, a symbiosis, union, and cooperation. We begin to assess how to create harmony and a working relationship between mind and body.

We ask ourselves: *What do I need to clear out of my mind, body, energy, environment, and relationships? What do I need less of?* Conversely, we ask ourselves: *What do I need to invite into my mind, body, energy, environment, and relationships? What do I need more of?*

Our Hare, a totem of shapeshifting, fast movement, and change, reminds us that we can create balance quickly and swiftly. The Germanic Goddess Eostre, who is the namesake of this festival, enjoyed the companionship of the Moon Hare, who laid eggs for children, gifting them the potentiality of their innocence and creativity, nourishment for the playfulness, curiosity, and discovery of the inner child. In the same way, at the Quarter Moon phase of the lunar cycle, we connect with the plans of our blueprint through internal self-discovery and curiosity. This is the pre-ovulation phase of the menstrual cycle where there is a need for nourishment and energy cultivation, in preparation for rapid Oestrogen rise, action, and bloom (at ovulation).

The ancient symbol of the Cosmic Egg is coded with the common mythos that the Great Mother Goddess who created the Universe, was the form of an egg, from which emerged the sun and moon. And so, within Goddess (and so within Sacred Woman) is totality, shadow and light, masculine and feminine, earth and cosmos, logic and intuition, night and day, death, and birth. Within Goddess, within us, is *all.* We hold tension in perfect union, amalgamating paradox.

What resilience and power Sacred Woman has!

Movement, cleaning out, and creativity are important aspects of this festival. Reclaiming and re-enacting 'childhood' activities – such as egg decorating, tying ribbons to sticks and dancing with them, and growing spring bulbs – can re-spark play and fun and innocent creativity for pleasure's sake. Going on a forest walk, or to a waterfall, to look for the Fae, fairies, and hugging a tree or playing stone skimming on water, are especially potent at this time and our inner Maiden loves to do these.

Most of all, we need to ground, breathe, and hydrate to support the next part of the cycle and integration of *all* into our being.

Your Body, Nervous System, and Energy in March

March is the time to connect with Nature. To ground into the electromagnetic grid of Gaia. It is time to deepen your relationship with kundalini and eros and start to move into and through the body for renewal. It is time to come into relationship with your root chakra (Mujadara which translates as root and support) to start to calm the sympathetic nervous system to ground into Gaia, to cultivate belonging, safety, and security and receive her abundance and stabilisation. In this module, you are also going to become aware of and develop a relationship with your perineum, anus, base of your spine and pelvis.

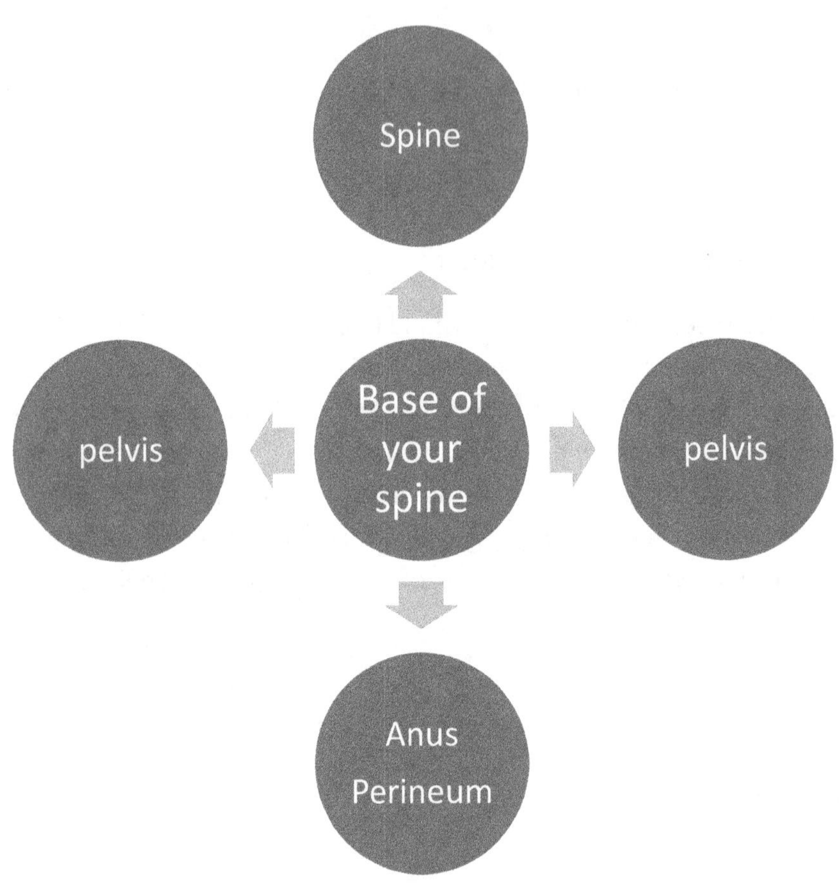
Spine
pelvis
Base of your spine
pelvis
Anus
Perineum

BODY

- Go outside for at least 30 minutes each day.

- Increase the amount of fluids you drink. Hydrate with pure, filtered water. Aim to drink a minimum of two litres of water each day.

- Do the 6-6-6 breathing and stilling exercise from the Rainbow Centre Diamond module. Breathe in through the nose into the rib cage for the count of 6. Hold your breath for count of 6. Exhale out of the mouth, down through the body, releasing the stomach muscles and softening your pelvic floor for the count of six. Do this exercise every day for at least five minutes.

- Get to know your body. It is empowering and useful to use a mirror to look at every part of your body and to touch all parts of your body. Note: it is totally normal for any area of your body to have hair on it!

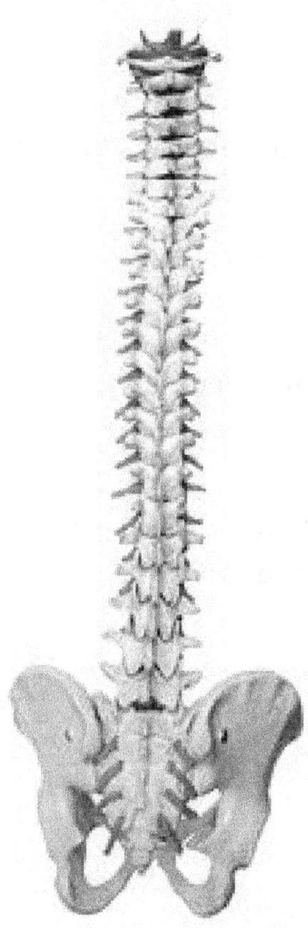

Anus: This is a sensitive and, believe it or not, potentially sexually pleasurable area of the body. It is the end of the digestive processing of the body, the intestine. It is the area from which we excrete, emptying the bowels.

Perineum: The super sensitive area of the body between the anus and vulva. Gentle touch of the perineum can be very pleasurable and sexually arousing. This is an amazing area to explore.

Base of the Spine: The base of the spine and the central nervous system is in an area of the lower back called the sacrum. At the very bottom is a fused set of bones called the coccyx, like a tail. If you run your finger from your vulva, back over your perineum and anus and into the small of your back you have reached the sacrum.

The Pelvis: Is the bone cradle which holds all the above.

NERVOUS SYSTEM

Do this **ABC exercise** focusing especially on the bottom and pelvis at least once each day.

This exercise reduces dissociation, brings us into the present, and supports the parasympathetic nervous system.

A: Anchor
Take your thoughts to your feet, bottom, and hips.
Let them feel heavy and connected to the ground and chair if you are sitting down.

B: Breathe
Breathe into your mind and then out through the body, down the legs
and out through the soles of the feet. Do this three times.

C: Contact
Put your hand on your body where the sensation of the emotion is most strongly felt – this may be your stomach, heart, or arms.

When contacting your body, speak kindly to it. Phrases like 'I see you' and 'I hear you' are helpful.

ENERGY: Root Chakra

Dominant in first seven years of life.

The blood red wheel and energy vortex located at the base of the spine, perineum, and anus. Visualising this supports the energy there to clear and enhance.

Placing your hands on your perineum and repeating the mantra, 'I am safe and secure in my body. I belong' will also support this chakra to strengthen.

Squatting and breathing out deeply through the mouth clear stagnation in this chakra.

When in balance this chakra offers us feelings of belonging, strong lifeforce and survival instincts, deep trust that our basic needs will be met, vitality, safety, concentration, clarity, love, and freedom.

When out of balance we may experience trauma, lack of connection, adrenal, intestinal, kidney, bone, and blood issues, feeling stuck, anxiety, rage, and ancestral dysfunction.

The root chakra teaches us that we are the tree of life. We are Goddess in the Middle World. The root chakra anchors Soul into human form and shows us the vital importance of embodiment.

- Tree hug. Sit on the ground at the base of a tree.
- Anchor at your perineum. Place in a grounding cord into the centre of the earth.
- Wrap your arms and legs around the tree.
- Inhale Gaia's energy and red dragon blood through your grounding cord and up the tree roots into your pelvis. Exhale and feel a stronger connection at the perinium and anus with the ground.

Do all of these for at least five minutes.

Working with your logical mind to assess and create balance.

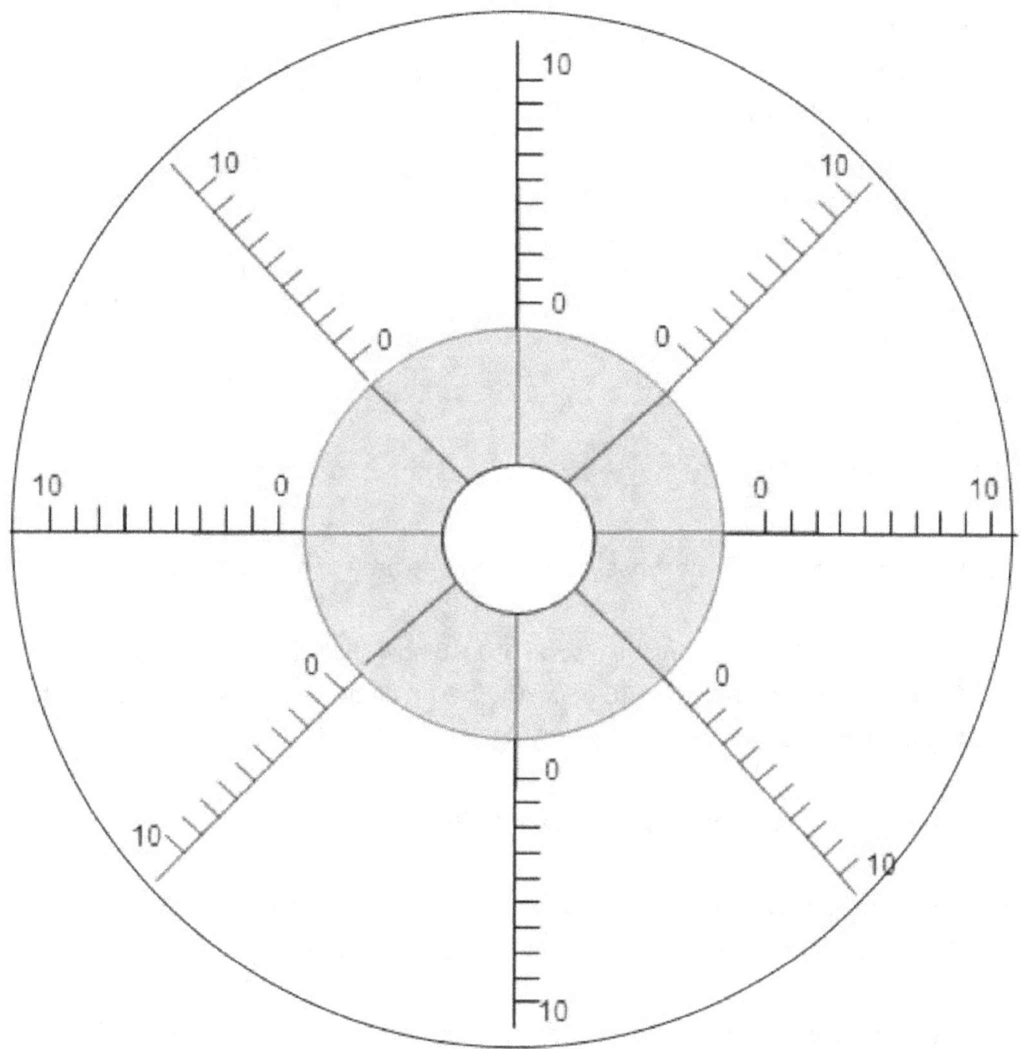

At Ostara, your logical mind and intuition work together supporting you to implement change to create balance. Thinking about your thinking – *metacognition* – is important. This life audit is a logical and structured method of assessing your current life situation and supporting you to ascertain priorities and where to implement change.

Instructions:

1. List eight areas of your life to assess. Here are some examples to choose from:
   - Family
   - Friends
   - Intimate Relationship
   - Work
   - Study
   - Finances
   - Physical Health
   - Sexuality
   - Mental Health
   - Social Media Use
   - Home
   - Fun
   - Creativity
   - Spirituality
   - Personal Growth

2. Label each section of the wheel above with one area of assessment.

3. Without overthinking, rank on a scale of 1-10 how that area of life is going/working for you. 0 being terribly and 10 being the best it could be. Draw a line across the segment for that rating.

4. Do this process for each segment/area of life.

5. Once you have completed it – look at your wheel which carries you through life. *How do you feel? How smoothly are you moving through life? Is your ride uneven?*

6. Answer these questions to dig deeper and to start to ascertain your priorities for where and how to create change:

   - *Which areas would you most like to change?*
   - *What would it be like if that area rated as 10?*
   - *What one change can you make in that area to increase the rating by 1 point?*
   - *Which changes can you make on your own?*
   - *Which changes need support and where can you source this from?*
   - *Where and why do you want to start with change?*

7. Set some intentions based on your answers for the next lunation.

Making a WAND

Creating this Magical Tool with Brigid, Nature, and the Four Elements.

Developing your intuition, creativity, and playfulness.

At the festival of Ostara, we connect to playfulness and reclaim our inner child. Our inner child, our Maiden, is *fully connected* to nature and the four elements, and is completely at one with magic. She is our magical Self, the aspect of Sacred Woman who sees, hears, feels, and knows magic everywhere.

The four elements – earth, air, fire, and water – are the building blocks of nature, of all life and creation, and the basis of all magic. A Wand is a magical tool which is used for channelling eros, inspiration, and focusing – and directing magic to amplify intention, bless and manifest. In making your own Wand you reactivate your own magic, infuse the tool with your own power and energy, remember your blueprint, and reclaim the power of Goddess.

Going forward throughout the year (every First Quarter Moon and pre-ovulation) your Maiden is predominant in your energy field and your inner child is very active. She wants you to be infused with, and play with magic, directly in relation to nature, to create renewal, to plan and fill with eros (alongside the oestrogen rise and the waxing moon), ready for creations to be birthed through you. Your Wand will be a useful support during this phase of your cycles.

What you need:

A collection of objects you were called to pick up whilst on walks in nature, in the forest or from a beach:

- A stick – which will be your wand (earth)
- Pebbles or stones
- Shells (water)
- Feathers (air)
- A candle (fire)
- Sage stick for smudging
- Matches
- Glue
- Scissors
- Ribbon, string
- Any other natural objects or items you'd like to decorate your wand with

Creating your wand:

- Burn some sage to smudge/energetically clear the area you are creating the wand in.

- Make sure you will be undisturbed.

- Take three deep breaths. Make sure you are 'in' your body.

- Ground and root yourself into Gaia's womb.

- Place your hand on your womb and forehead and think about the power you'd like your wand to be infused with.

- Then create three intentions you'd like for your wand.

- Call forth the power of Goddess, Brigid, Earth, Air, Fire, Water, Gaia and the power of your womb, heart, and mind.

- Create and decorate your wand.

- Activate your wand immediately (see below).

Activating your wand:

- Hold your wand over your womb and say, 'By the power of my blood I activate my wand with…' and say your three intentions out loud.

- Hold your wand over your heart and say, 'By the power of my love I activate my wand with…' and say your three intentions out loud.

- Hold your wand over your forehead and say, 'By the power of my sight I activate my wand with…' and say your three intentions out loud.

- Point your wand to the Earth and say, 'By the power of Gaia I activate and fill my wand with the blood, lifeforce, eros and Dragon power of the earth.'

- Point your wand to the Sky and say, 'By the power of the cosmos I activate and fill my wand with the consciousness, inspiration, and power of the air.'

- Point your wand at the candle and say, 'By the power of Brigid I activate and fill my wand with the power of the triple flame of fire.'

- Place some of your saliva on the wand and say, 'By the power of my DNA I activate and fill my wand with the power of water.'

- Then say, 'It is done' three times and, 'So it is' three times and then finish by saying, 'This is for the highest good of all.'

Store your wand safely with your cloth bag of crystals. Use it when crystal gridding, doing ceremony, grounding, or setting intentions.

Painting by Kat Shaw

Introduction to Orange Module

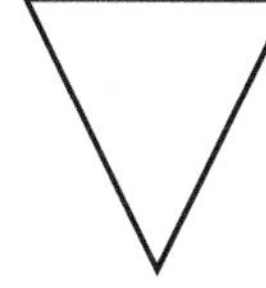 

KEY CONCEPTS TO INTEGRATE:

LOVER: Relational, passionate, and emotional aspect of Self which gives us access to physical joy, bliss, and intimacy.

WOMB SPACE: Sacral chakra. Area of the body just below the belly button, responsible for sexual, creative, and emotional energy.

WOMB: The uterus.

VULVA: Externally visible female genitalia.

MENARCHE: First menstrual bleed.

MENSTRUATION: (aka Moon Time or Period) Vaginal bleeding that occurs as a normal part of a woman's MENSTRUAL CYCLE when the uterus sheds its lining.

SEXUALITY: Power of sexual feelings, exploration, and activity.

SELF-PLEASURE: (aka masturbation, but that is not an exceptionally beautiful word) Exploring and stimulating your body sexually for your OWN pleasure, satisfaction, and enjoyment.

PLEASURE: Enjoyment, delight, fun.

DESIRE: Longing, aspiration, wish.

PASSION: Hunger, enthusiasm, intensity.

RITUAL: Ceremony, act, practice

EMOTION: Energy in motion, instinctive and intuitive knowing.

Month: May

Season: Late Spring/Early Summer

Festival: Beltane

Direction: South-East

Element: Air

Goddess archetype: LOVER – Goddess Aphrodite

Symbol: Downward triangle

Animal: Serpent

Moon: Waxing Gibbous

Menstrual: Pre-ovulation

Body area: Vulva and Womb

Chakra: Sacral

Crystal: Carnelian (creativity, vitality, courage, sexual energy)

Oil: Clary Sage (womb and menstrual health, stress, anxiety, digestive support)

In this module you will connect to your LOVER and WOMB SPACE, your WOMB itself and VULVA, the most powerful, passionate, and creative parts of Self, where universal and earth energies take up residence within your body. Within the womb space we receive and vision, form and gestate, and then birth. The frequency of your Lover also channels eros and transmutes the erotic energy into embodied bliss and pleasure, as you intimately relate to yourself, as well as others. Your Lover initiates you onto the Sacred Womanhood path, via your MENARCHE, the onset of your MENSTRUAL CYCLE, and shows you the wisdom and potency of your blood each MENSTURATION.

Connection to your SEXUALITY is integral to this module. Through SELF-PLEASURE you explore and stimulate your body sexually for your OWN PLEASURE, satisfaction, and enjoyment. Going forward, connection and union with another is now more carefully assessed. You only want someone who gives you even more bliss, joy, and love! You become powerful and more in touch with your DESIRE and PASSION. You know what you want and where to go to get it. You attract love from others who are 'healthy' because you have filled yourself up first, so are no longer needy, and couple only with those who do the same. Love, respect for your body image, and self-care are anchored and integrated into your life.

The element of air at Beltane fans the flames of eros within your womb as the frenzy of sexual urges rise and the longing for pleasure and to conceive is paramount. In listening to your body, the wisdom of the sexuality and the menstrual cycle, and engaging in sensual RITUAL, you start to experience more mastery of EMOTION and self-awareness. During this module you become conscious of how energy, soul, and Goddess fuse with your blood, emotional self, and sexuality – anchoring PLEASURE as the foundation of your Sacred Womanhood incarnation.

LOVER – Goddess Aphrodite

Aphrodite is the Greek Goddess of sexuality. She had many god and human lovers and through their unions, Light shone. Her Goddess qualities include love and beauty, and she gifts us passion, pleasure, and the ability to create. One of the greatest stories surrounding Aphrodite was her birthing of the god Eros through her union with the god Ares. Childbirth and mothering, however, are not her primary characteristics or gifts to us. She creates a loving coupling with a deeply joyful sensuality and desire of self. She reminds us that our bodies are vehicles for self-pleasure and sexuality which can be enjoyed in and of itself, for our own pleasure's sake. We are the aphrodisiac of and for ourselves.

Take a moment to reflect on this and your relationship with desire and sexual pleasure. What comes up for you?

Welcome to May. The season of Orange. The Earth is moist and fertile and so are we. Lifeforce is abundantly flowing, and we are full of expectation. Spring is in full force; summer is on the horizon, and we can feel its heat rising in our bodies. We are feeling turned on, aroused, and alive. We have an abundance of energy. There is more sunlight, the days are quickly getting longer, and energy increases rapidly. We move into a place of feeling uninhibited, rampant, and feral.

The festival of Beltane falls on the wheel of the year halfway between Ostara and Litha, the Summer Solstice. The calendared date for the festival is May 1st, May Day. At this festival there is a longing to come into union, make love, and experience the pleasure and power of eros; energetically, physically, mentally, and spiritually. This is the festival of the LOVER – of DESIRE and PLEASURE – and a coming together of paradox and polarity – of Flesh and Energy, Mind and Body, Self and Other, Self-pleasure and Spiritual Love. As they fuse, creation and manifestation occur through ECSTASY.

Love is literally in the Air which fans the flames of passion. Our wild Self, the sexually potent and untamed Goddess, needs to express and be satisfied, and our ancestors honoured this. They performed sexual acts outside on the night of Beltane, in dedication to the fertility and creativity of the land, they bathed in the wild waters and wells, honouring the elements, elementals, and nature Spirits. There would be dancing with ribbons around the Maypole phallus, weaving the masculine and feminine into union, to create and continue Life and Birth. Finally, as Beltane marked the start of the fire season, ancestors would light fires which the community would then leap over to celebrate the return of the waxing sun and to cleanse, purify and invite fertility and birth for the village, crops, and livestock.

During this month we ask ourselves: *What blocks do I need to clear out of my mind, body, energy, environment, and relationships to create space for MORE and MORE PLEASURE? What do I need less of?* Conversely, we ask ourselves: *What do I need to invite into my mind, body, energy, environment, and relationships? What do I need more of? What needs to happen for me to reclaim the POWER of my womb, sexuality, and body?*

Our Serpent is one of the oldest archetypes and symbols of the power of the Feminine and sexual energy. The Serpent can be depicted as the Ouroboros, the earth dragon of the underworld, eating its tail in an egg-shaped cyclical movement, a totem of immortality and the continual death and rebirth, shedding and renewal due to the shedding of skins and echoes a woman's menstrual cycle.

The serpent is also a symbol of eros, Gaia's energy and kundalini, all of which rise strongly within us just prior to ovulation. This is a phase of the menstrual cycle, just prior to ovulation where our Oestrogen peaks. We are bright, glowing, and ready to 'mate' deeply with ourselves and with others and to be penetrated by BLISS, RAPTURE and experience deep sexual pleasure and ecstasy. Similarly, at the Waxing Gibbous phase of the lunar cycle we also experience these energies more strongly and can connect and create union with ease, implement strategy and plans, make love to new projects, and fertilise them – knowing they'll be birthed at full moon.

The ancient symbol of the downward triangle, the Yoni Yantra, is representative of the Goddess within, our Shakti energy and area of the body which in its entirety is the pubic area, the womb space and vulva area. It is a symbol of yin, the bottom triangle of the first three chakras, and is coded with concepts such as cyclical wisdom, trinity, triple goddess, love, sexual power, conception, birthing, completion, love, and power.

What power the womb space of Sacred Woman has!

Rapid growth happens this month. Nature is rampant and swelling. Being outside as much as possible is encouraged so nature can mentor you. Sitting and grounding near a Hawthorn tree expands your heart energy and there are many herbs and plants available at this time of year to make teas and essences from. Eat local produce and pick some wildflowers for your area – and place them in your home to deeply connect you to the land, energy, and part of Gaia's body you are living in.

Most of all, this month you will EXPLORE body and release sexual pleasure from shame, cultivating body love and positivity.

Your Body, Nervous System, and Energy in May

May is the time to connect with libido, sexual, and sensual energy – to feel and unite with Gaia's frenzied erotic spiral through the soles of your feet, perineum, and vagina into your womb. It is time to deepen your relationship with kundalini and bliss – transforming into orgasmic ecstasy if you choose. It is time to bond with your sacral chakra (Svadhisthana, which translates as sweetness) to start to stabilise the sympathetic nervous system through pleasure – through the sacral chakra we receive. In this module, you are also going to become aware of and develop an affiliation with your vulva and blood, cutting the cords with shame around these.

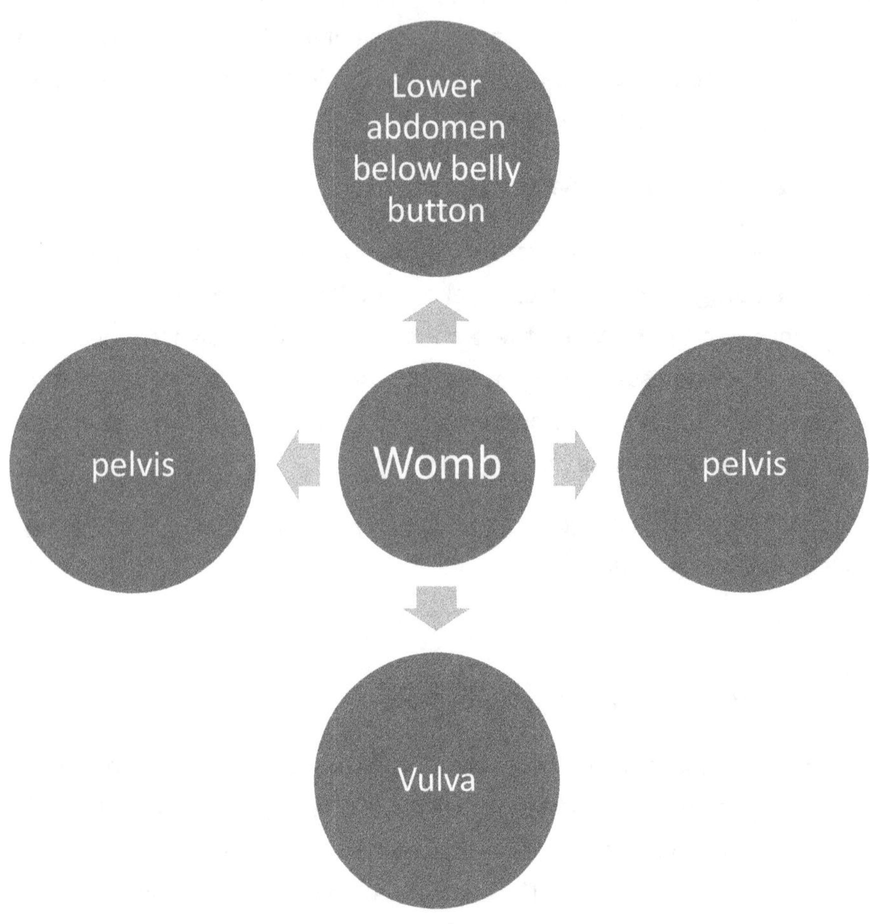

Lower abdomen below belly button
pelvis
Womb
pelvis
Vulva

BODY

- Go outside for at least 45 minutes each day.

- Continue to drink plenty of fluids but also introduce orange foods into your diet. Oranges, carrots, sweet potato, and melon are good examples.

- Do the butterfly yoga posture daily.

Sit on the floor with the soles of the feet together.

Feel your perineum against the floor. Put in a grounding cord.

Clasp your feet with your hands.

Push your chest forward until your feel your back gently stretch.

Hold and inhale. Pause the breath.

Exhale, bringing the chest back to the neutral starting position.

Continue this moving forward and back for at least five minutes.

Notice how it feels in your womb space and the energy which is generated.

- Make a womb space dance list for yourself. Freely dance moving every part of your body with no expectation other than pleasure!

- Connect to your menstrual blood. Touch it, smell it. Recognise that THIS is the POWER of creation, of life.

- Connect to your menstrual cycle. Listen to your body.

- Get to know your VULVA – all parts. It is empowering and useful to use a mirror to look at every part of your body and to touch all parts of your body. Remember: It is totally normal for any area of your body to have hair on it!

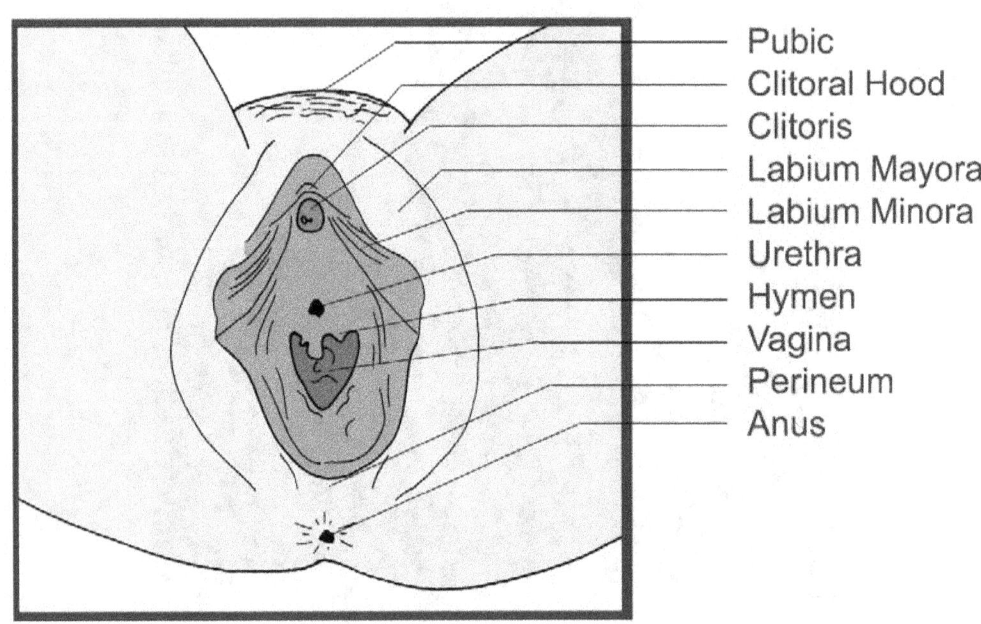

(Image credit: Wikimedia Commons)

Pubic mound: mound of Venus.

Clitoral hood: tissue protection for the clitoris.

Clitoris: engorges with blood during sexual arousal – its function is sexual pleasure.

Vagina: hidden from view by outer lips (labia majora) – visible when inner lips (labia minora) are spread. This is the area of penetration and where menstrual blood or a baby at birth exits the body.

Urethra: from which we urinate.

Hymen: membrane inside the entrance of the vagina.

NERVOUS SYSTEM

Do this **Vulva breathing** exercise daily to increase body positivity, desire, passion, and your capacity for pleasure.

Sit on the floor with the soles of your feet together. Lean back supported by your arms and hands, palms down behind you.

Rock your pelvis.

Let your legs fall open.

Continue to rock the pelvis with your legs open.

Breathe in as you rock forward and push out your chest.

Breathe out as you rock back.

Continue for at least five minutes. Focus on your vulva and use breath to create energy there and in the womb. Allow the rhythm of the movement and your breath to soothe and calm.

ENERGY: Sacral Chakra

Dominant 8-14 years.

The orange wheel and energy vortex is located within the uterus, womb, and lower abdomen, below the belly button. Visualising this supports the energy there to clear and enhance.

Place your hands on your womb and repeat the mantra, 'I trust, embrace, and welcome the pleasure and sacredness of sexuality. I honour, love, and respect my body temple and its creative force will also support this chakra to strengthen.'

Stand up and make the shape of the Yoni Yantra – downward triangle – on your womb space, whilst moving the hips in a figure of eight and breathing in and out deeply from the perineum. This will also support the body to connect more powerfully to pleasure and lifeforce.

When in balance, this chakra offers us feelings of flow, pleasure, trust in the cycles of life, harmony, nurturance, flexibility, freedom, fun.

When out of balance, we may experience emotional extremes – such as rage and chronic anxiety, shame, menstrual and abdominal, pelvic issues and pain, low or high libido, blocked creativity, and difficulty expressing needs and emotions.

The sacral chakra teaches us that our body is the portal of all creation. We are Goddess in the Middle world. The sacral chakra anchors the cosmos and eros into human form and shows us the vital importance of pleasure and sexuality as forms of creative power.

Self-pleasure, sexual self-touch and masturbation are a safe and totally normal way to feel good, to love your body, and to feel powerful in your body and positive in your body. Self-pleasure helps you get to know what turns you on and arouses you.

Take your time to stroke, touch, rub (gently), and explore all areas of your body, including the vulva, the breasts, and the nipples of your body. It's nice to bathe, light a candle, and listen to some music as part of this.

Allow your imagination and mind to do what it wants, follow the sensations of the body – be curious, explore what you enjoy, and let the body lead the process.

You cannot get it wrong. Goddess knows how and what will make you feel good.

GROUND

- Sit on the ground and cup your vulva in your hands. Put in your grounding cord and breathe in eros, Gaia's energy, through your perineum and vulva. Fill up your womb space. Exhale out of the sacral chakra, front and back of your body, the orange wheel just below the belly button.

- Do this for at least five minutes.

Know yourself! Write a diary entry for each day of your menstrual cycle for 3-6 months.

Day 1 is the first day of your bleed and the last day of your cycle is the day before the next bleed.

Make notes and rank these days on a scale of 1-10 (0 feels terrible – 10 feels amazing) how you feel each day:

- Physically
- Emotionally
- Sexually
- Mentally
- Energy
- Mood

Also, keep track of what you notice about vaginal fluids and secretions. This is important, as just before ovulation these become more wet, slippery, and stretchy like raw egg white. Fertility and the chance of getting pregnant are higher the four days before and after the egg is released.

After a few months, you will notice patterns and become more confident on 'bad' days. When you aren't feeling great, know that this will soon change, and you will feel well and upbeat again. You will become more resilient. You will be able to schedule your time; what to eat, who to see, and what to do, according to your body's unique cycle.

This is the power of knowing your body and living as a cyclical Sacred Woman.

Know Your Internal Womb

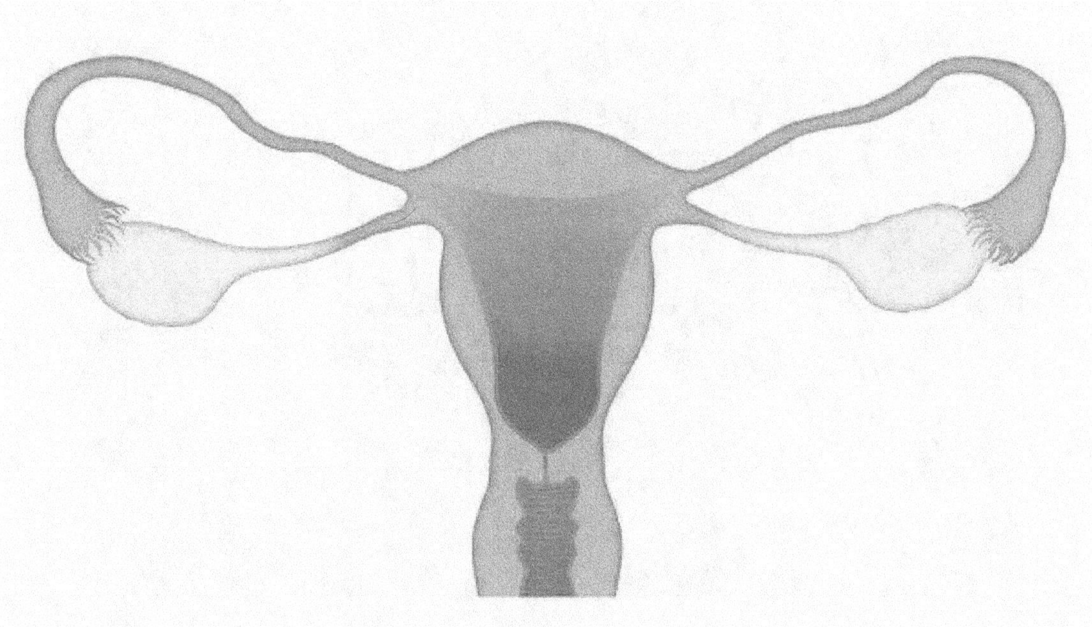

Egg tubes/Fallopian tubes: Eggs pass from the ovaries along these tubes into the uterus.

Ovaries: Store of human eggs. Monthly, they mature and release an egg which is moved from the ovary to fimbriae (at the end of the fallopian tube) via waves of fluid created by the finger fringes at the end.

Uterus: The womb and area where a baby grows. Contains various tissues – endometrium which sheds and renews with menstrual cycle; myometrium – smooth muscle which contracts during menstruation and childbirth; and perimetrium – protective shell or membrane for other layers.

Cervix: Tip of the uterus, opening at the os, where sperm enters the uterus and through which blood or a baby leave.

Vagina: A canal, approximately four inches long, full of ridges, called rugea.

PLEASURE BATH RITUAL

SELF CARE MAGIC FOR YOUR BODY TEMPLE

Developing SELF-LOVE and BODY-POSITIVITY. MANIFESTING through PLEASURE.

At the festival of Beltane, we connect to our Lover. We realise that we are MORE THAN THOUGHT. We are pure embodiment of raw primal libido and life force, uncontrollable – a force which creates, gestates, and births. This area is the womb space and connecting through touch to that area channels and intentionalises our power even more, creating body positivity and image. We start to appreciate and really FEEL body love.

Touching the body consciously can be a new ritual for us, and through touch we activate and strengthen our magic. Sexuality and self-pleasure are a manifesting force and orgasm creates an explosion of creatrix power. We are co-creating with Gaia, the Cosmos and Life itself. This needs to be done mindfully and with clear intention, respect, and reverence.

Claiming growth through pleasure, body positivity, and self-love is a revolutionary and political act. The body can feel fear during the process, so go slowly. LOVE and care for all aspects of Self.

Going forward throughout the year – at every Waxing Gibbous Moon and/or just prior to ovulation – your Lover is predominant in your energy field and your erotic self is highly active. She wants you to be infused by, and play with, sexual energy to create bliss, ecstasy, and self-pleasure – so you create, birth, learn and change with enjoyment, love, and satisfaction. Not through pain. Pleasure baths are a ritual to anchor into your magic toolbox, routine, and monthly planning.

If you do not have a bath, you can do a pleasure shower ritual instead, placing the flowers in a vase and adding essential oils to a salt scrub.

What you need:

- A collection of wild or bought flowers

- Your favourite essential oils (definitely recommend using clary sage)

- Epsom salts

- Your carnelian crystal

- Any other favourite crystals

- Some chocolate

- A glass of iced water with lemon and/or fresh mint

- Clean towel

- Your favourite body lotion

- A candle

- Sage stick for smudging

- Matches

- Glue

- Notebook

- Pen

Creating your pleasure bath:

- Light your candle.

- Burn some sage to smudge and energetically clear the area you are creating the wand in.

- Make sure you will be undisturbed.

- Take three deep breaths. Make sure you are 'in' your body.

- Ground and root yourself into Gaia's womb.

- Run your bath mindfully and give thanks to the cleaning and birthing power of the element of water. Add the flowers, salts, your crystal, and oils, giving thanks to Gaia as you do this.

- Place your hand on your womb and forehead and determine the magic you would like your bath to be infused with. Love, bliss, pleasure – anything else? You choose!

- Then create three intentions you would like to manifest from your bath and through the pleasure of your body.

- Call forth the power of Goddess, Aphrodite, Earth, Air, Fire, Water, Gaia and the power of your womb, heart, and mind.

- Get into the bath.

- Activate your bath immediately (see below).

Activating your ritual pleasure bath:

- Hold your hand over your womb and say, 'By the power of my blood I activate my ritual bath with…' and say your three intentions out loud.

- Hold your hand over your heart and say, 'By the power of my love I activate my ritual bath with…' and say your three intentions out loud.

- Hold your hand over your forehead and say, 'By the power of my mind I activate my ritual bath with…' and say your three intentions out loud.

- Place your hands in the water and say, 'By the power of Aphrodite I activate my ritual bath with the power of pleasure, lifeforce and flow.'

- Point your hand to the Sky and say, 'By the power of the cosmos I activate my ritual bath with the consciousness, inspiration and power of the air.'

- Point your hand at the candle and say, 'By the power of the sun and heat I activate and fill my bath with the power of the flames of fire.'

- Place one finger on your vagina say, 'By the power of my blood and sexual fluids I activate and fill my ritual bath with the power of pleasure and creative power, with the power of Goddess embodied within me.'

- Then say, 'It is done' three times and, 'So it is' three times, and then finish by saying, 'This is for the highest good of all.'

During your time in your bath, sip the water, slowly suck the chocolate. Make a downward triangle shape on your womb space on your body with your hands. Breathe into this area and lightly stroke your whole body with your fingertips, spending extra time at your stomach, belly button, womb space, and vulva. Do the vulva breathing exercises from earlier in this module. Explore your vulva, touch your clitoris. Dream. Vision. Listen to your body. Speak to your body kindly.

When you come out of the bath dry yourself with your warmed clean towel. Mindfully, slowly and sensually apply body lotion. Feel the pleasure of touching and stroking your skin.

If you feel aroused, self-pleasure yourself. Hold your intentions and ask them to manifest through the power of your arousal and orgasm, if that is part of the experience.

Store your oils and crystal in your cloth magical tool kit bag.

If you want to dig deeper, you may also enjoy the ***Making Love with the Divine: Sacred, Ecstatic, Erotic Experiences*** workbook and online programme: https://thegirlgod.com/courseofferings.php

Painting by Kat Shaw

Introduction to Yellow Module

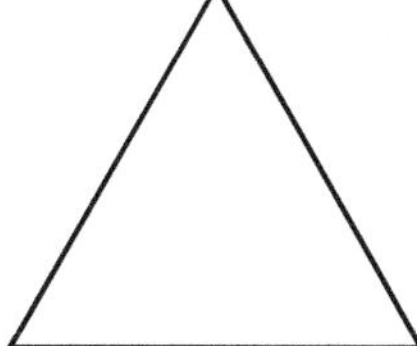 

KEY CONCEPTS TO INTEGRATE:

WARRIORESS: a woman who is a warrior.

HUNTRESS: a woman who is a hunter.

POWER: sovereignty, capacity, capability.

ALLIANCE: union, partnership.

EXPRESSION: communication, demonstration.

SOLAR FEMININE: light feminine, sun Goddess.

WORTH: value.

BIRTHING: bearing, manifesting into form.

WILL: desire, wish, ambition, determination.

MIND: intellect, psyche, awareness.

RESILIENCE: flexibility, elasticity, bounciness.

EMOTIONAL MASTERY: capacity to be with emotions.

UPPER WORLD: the cosmos and womb of Sophia (Goddess Wisdom).

Month: June

Season: Summer

Festival: Litha

Direction: South

Element: Fire

Goddess archetype: WARRIORESS/HUNTRESS – Goddess Athena

Symbol: Upward Triangle

Animal: Lioness

Moon: Full Moon

Menstrual: Ovulation

Body area: Stomach, Liver, Kidney, and Adrenals

Chakra: Solar Plexus

Crystal: Catrine (prosperity, abundance, joy, success, enthusiasm, self-esteem, self-confidence, brain power)

Oil: Cypress (vitality, energy, skin health, renewal, uplift, grounding, motivation, stress reduction)

In this module you will connect with your WARRIORESS, your HUNTRESS and your SOLAR PLEXUS (your POWER centre). This is the place of the SOLAR FEMININE, WORTH and WILL within your body. It is also the area from which you develop RESILIENCE, BOUNDARIES and MASTERY, the place where EMOTIONAL digestion happens. The frequency of your Warrioress also assists you in your BIRTHING processes. Your Warrioress and Huntress also initiate you into your Sacred Womanhood, via your ovulation, and through your willingness to be seen, to expand, to assert your will, say no and self-protect.

Connection to your WILL and courage is integral to this module. Through ALLIANCE with your own truth and desires, you call on UPPER WORLD support, merging your will with Divine will, and birthing your deepest longings into form. By accepting your body's enjoyment of the hunt and roar, the majesty of your Lioness comes alive within you, and you seek and pursue for your own interests and meet your needs and desires. In doing so, you become more attentive to your emotions, and mother yourself. Your sense of self WORTH is activated and as you follow your impulse and lifeforce you consent to your body's lead and position the MIND as a tool you can use to strategize and implement the body's instinctual knowing. You cultivate courage and movement in this module. You learn how to shine brightly and harvest with the FULL MOON, the sun and the SOLAR FEMININE. The element of fire is active, strong, and hot within womb, heart, and mind in this module. Eros and Gaia's lifeforce climax.

During this module you become conscious of how you can work with and channel energy to co-create and merge your own divine will for manifestation.

WARRIORESS/HUNTRESS – Goddess Athena

Athena is the Greek Goddess of war, protection, and practical creativity. She is often pictured with an owl which represents her wisdom – sometimes an olive branch representing her focus on freedom – or a spear representing her warrior and hunting qualities and skills. She is thought to have remained a virgin, sovereign in her own body, and so she reminds us that all aspects of ourselves – our mind, body, heart, and energy belong first and foremost to us – and can be offered through the service and activities we choose to engage in or protect.

In being fully dependent on her own internal wisdom and resources, she mentors us in resilience, emotional mastery and assertiveness – and the importance of knowing and following our own goals, desires and will. She is thought to have been a great planner and strategist, so she offers us allyship with our mind, creating union between mind, body, and heart, so they all work together for us, not against us. In doing so, like her, we can lead others into and through empowerment in the name of the greatest good.

Take a moment to reflect on this and your relationship with your own inner knowing, willpower, and resilience. How are they working for you?

Welcome to June. The season of Yellow. The Earth is in her full climax, glory, and expansiveness, and so are we. The Sun is at its maximum brilliance, brightness, and heat. Summer is fully here, and we have attained all we were meant to learn, experience, and grow this wheel of the year. We are incarnated, hot and in union. Our energy levels and erotic drive are at their peak. Light is everywhere. Although there is little darkness, we now accept that night will start to advance again. We are joyful and flowing in the fullness of Self.

The festival of Litha, the Summer Solstice, occurs when the wheel of the year pauses, halfway between Beltane and Lammas. The calendared date for the festival is June 21st. On this mid summer's eve, daylight is dominant as we experience the longest day and shortest night. Every part of nature is in full bloom, flourishing and radiant. We feel, along with Gaia, complete and powerful. We are fully expressive, resilient, and connected to ourselves and all of creation and the cosmos. We are allied and supported in gestating and strategising, planning, and implementing our unique gifts into form. This is the festival of the WARRIORESS & HUNTRESS – of POWER and WORTH – of UNION of mind and body, of INDIVIDUALITY. LITHA is about our WILL, intention, and goals. The Solar Feminine ensures we use our mind in a discerning way to ripen our wishes and desires in an emotionally balanced way.

Solar power and Gaia's erotic flow are literally the fires within us at this festival. Our proud and courageous Lioness self is ready to roar, be heard, and be seen. Clarity of intention and personal will are vital at this festival as we channel solar rays of manifestation in alignment and accordance with what we want to harvest in the autumn, inwardly and outwardly. This festival is about being visible so that movement and using your voice in your own way will support you to anchor the energetics into your mind, body, heart, womb, and energy field. Manifestation into the form of your dreams will continue through the times of harvest so we continue to complete projects and rebirth self throughout the summer and autumn.

Our ancestors deeply honoured the solar currents and clearly understood their potency. There was great celebration in communities. As at Beltane, huge bonfires were lit, usually of oak, and as described in the legend of the battle of the oak and holly king, it is the holly king who triumphs at this solstice. Members of the community jumped over the bonfires, inviting in love, fertility, and an abundant harvest. Wheels were a big part of this festival; circular candlelit processions took place, cartwheels rolled downhill, set ablaze, all inviting in the continuation and promise of life and rebirth, the return of the sun after the winter. This festival merged polarity, simultaneously celebrating the full expansion of the outer, of life, peak heat and sun whilst recognising the return of the inner darkness and death.

At summer solstice we ask ourselves: *What achievements am I celebrating? What blocks are keeping me from attaining my intentions – and what do I need to release?* Conversely, we ask ourselves: *What do I need to invite into my mind, body, energy to empower myself? What do I need more of? What needs to happen for me to express and expansively roar as all I am?*

Our Lioness is a symbol of the Solar Feminine, our hot nature. Her golden fur is a representation of the sun's ray. She is our protectress, warrioress and huntress, willing to be in the spotlight and be seen without shame. She will shatter any glass ceiling, move out of her comfort zone – independently providing all she needs for herself and ensuring she remains stable in battle or engagement. The Lioness is an icon of Divinity and of Queendom. She likes to hunt for her own survival and incarnation. She has autonomy of her body, deciding who to mate with, discerning where to share herself and her energy. She is the pillar of the family unit and radiates beauty and poise.

The ancient symbol of the upward triangle is representative of the 'active' principle – of 'doing' and the 'upper world' – traditionally linked with the 'masculine,' 'God' and penetrative sun energy. The upward triangle is a symbol of fire and of yang, consciousness, the upper triangle of the top three chakras (throat, third eye and crown), and is loaded with concepts such as rising, spiritual aspiration, thought, ascension, ambition, and manifestation.

Outdoor gatherings, socialising, celebrating, and performances (think of *A Midsummer Night's Dream*) are activities of this month. It is warm, days are long and it's a perfect time for this. Making a solar outdoor altar, decorating with gold items, oak leaves and flowers is a beautiful focus for working with intention and the sun. Placing water outside on the altar to infuse with the sun's rays – and then drinking or bathing in it – fills us up more deeply with the energy of the lioness and solar feminine. Roses tend to be abundant at this time and it is wonderful to smell their intoxicating scent, which reminds us of the seductiveness, beauty and worth of our own full bloom.

Most of all, we become focused and ensure that our will and actions are clearly aligned with our intentions and goals, and that those we are in alliance with are serving our highest good and manifestation. This month is about cultivating and strengthening the power of the mind.

Your Body, Nervous System, and Energy in June

June is the month to connect with your willpower, worth and resilience. It is an invitation of expansion and the drawing up of more erotic energy and lifeforce from Gaia. It is time to deepen your relationship with the fire, sun, and manifestation, through your own determination, drive, and resolve. It is time to come into relationship with your solar plexus (Manipura, which translates as city of gems) to begin to activate the sympathetic nervous system in a regulated, titrated, and manageable way and to cultivate assertiveness, self-representation and willpower. In this module you are also going to become aware of and develop a relationship with your stomach, your digestive fire, your liver, your kidneys, and adrenal glands. It is time to feel powerful, make decision, be independent, be self-disciplined and know your worth.

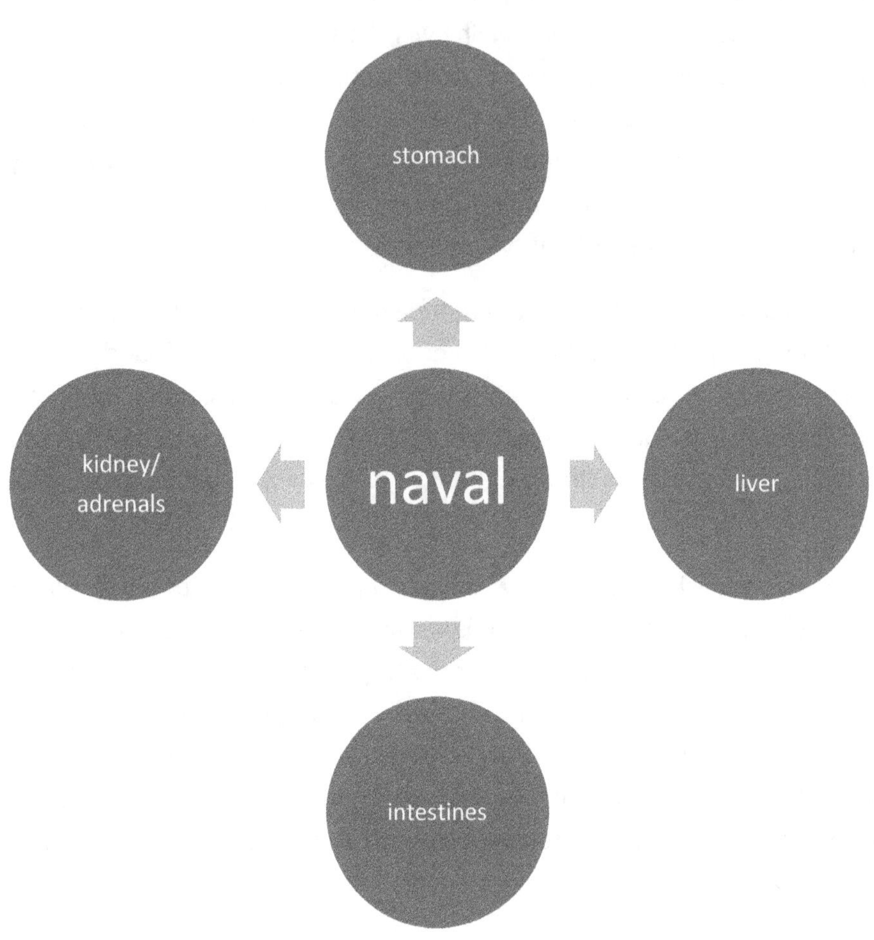

stomach
kidney/
adrenals
naval
liver
intestines

BODY

- Go outside for at least 1 hour each day.

- Continue to drink plenty of fluids but also introduce yellow foods into your diet. Melon, lemon, and yellow peppers are good examples.

- Mix some of the cypress essential oil with a carrier oil, such as fractionated coconut oil, and massage some at the base and top of your spine. This will ground, stabilise, and motivate your nervous system all at the same time.

- Do the fire breathing daily to balance the sympathetic nervous system, bolster concentration, and improve digestion.

Sit on the floor cross-legged, in an easy pose.

Feel your perineum against the floor. Put in a grounding cord.

Place your hands on your lap palms up.

Inhale and exhale strongly through the nose, contracting the stomach muscles.

The inhale and exhale need to be even with no pause.

Do for 10 seconds to start, build to 30 seconds.

Notice how it feels in your solar plexus and the power energy generated.

- Make a power and motivation music list for yourself. Listen to it and imagine yourself as a Queen.
- Connect to your digestion, how you urinate and excrete. Experiment with different foods. Track how you digest them – what works for your body and what does not. Reduce shame around this. When we excrete, we clear the body of toxins and toxic emotions. This process is vital for wellness.
- Get to know your STOMACH, LIVER, KIDNEY, and ADRENAL GLANDS – all parts.

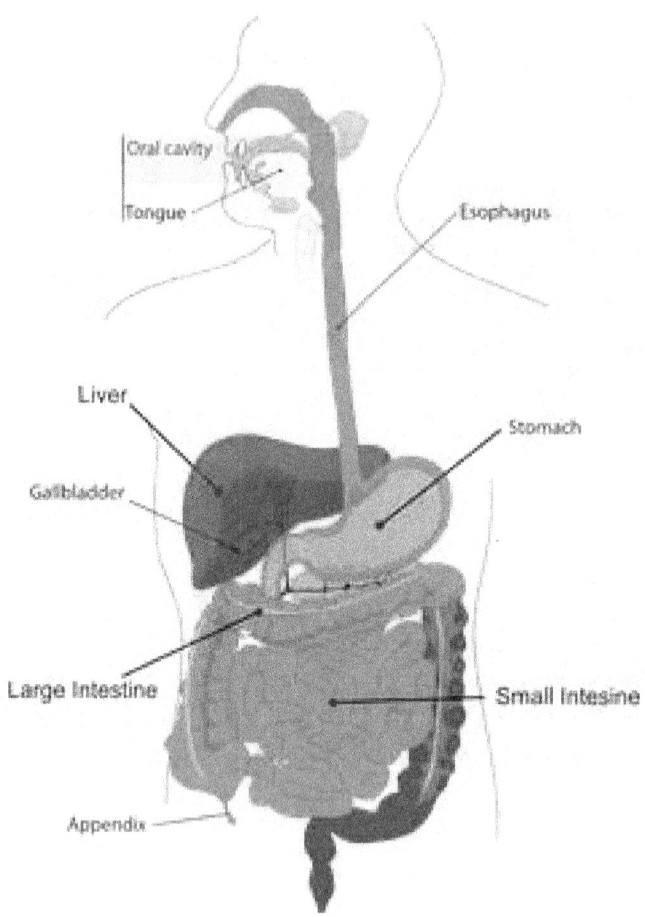

Stomach: On the left side of your upper torso. Food travels there for digestion. Contains enzymes and acid.

Liver: On the right side of your torso, under your rib cage. Supports food digestion and the elimination of toxins.

Kidneys: Two bean-shaped organs the size of fists which are situated at the back of the body, either side of the spine, just below the rib cage. Blood is filtered through them; waste and water are removed which makes urine.

Adrenals: Glands which sit like hats on top of each kidney which produce hormones and cortisol, a substance which helps us cope with stress.

NERVOUS SYSTEM

Stabilise the Kidney and Adrenal glands through self-touch and intention daily before you go to sleep.

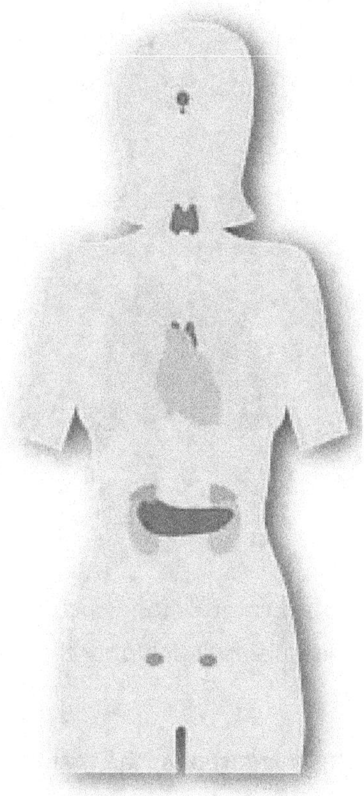

In bed, place your hands on the front of your body, either side of your torso under your rib cage. Imagine your back is floating on and is supported by a warm, salty sea.

As you touch your body, imagine that through the palms of your hands you are beaming calmness and understanding to your kidneys and adrenal glands. Send them the intention and message of it being safe to be calm, drop into the warm sea, relax, and let go.

Keep breathing deeply in and out, with your hands against your body.

Do this for five minutes each night.

ENERGY: Solar Plexus

Dominant 14-21 years.

The yellow wheel and energy vortex located within the upper torso, the area above the belly button where the diaphragm is. Visualising this supports the energy there to fortify and consolidate.

Place your hands on your upper belly and repeat the mantra, 'I am sovereign, powerful, worthy, and courageous. I know who I am, and where I am going. I self-lead and manifest, merging my will with divine will for the highest good' will also support this chakra to strengthen.'

Standing up and making the shape of the upward triangle on your stomach and then above your head – whilst breathing in and out deeply from the diaphragm – will also support the body to connect to your personal power and channel solar support.

When in balance, this chakra offers us assertiveness, harmonious relationships, manifestation of will and desires, clarity of mind, power, wisdom, and courage.

When out of balance, we may experience being over-controlling, micromanaging, helplessness, obsessiveness, manipulation, lack of clarity, inability to manifest – alongside digestive discomfort and chronic stress, fatigue and eating disorders.

The solar plexus chakra supports us to be empowered, to set boundaries and please ourselves, not others. We are Goddess of our own destiny. The solar plexus anchors the cosmos and sun into human form and shows us the vital importance of self-discipline and following our internal teacher and locus of control.

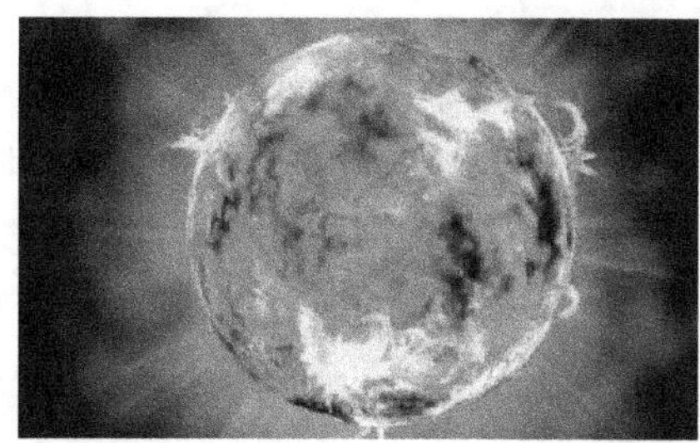

Experiment with channelling energy and creating power balls.

Breath in through your feet and the top of your head and bring the breath into the solar plexus to create a ball of yellow fire energy, a ball of sun energy.

Lift the ball of energy out of your stomach and take the breath though the palms of the hands until the balls of fire energy become the size of a football.

Decide how you want to use your power. You can throw the balls at situations you want to explosively change or destroy, and/or place the fire ball into situations or intentions you want to empower and grow.

You choose. Do this several times.

You cannot get it wrong. Goddess knows how to mentor you in this empowerment energy channelling.

GROUND

- Stand outside, feet planted firmly on the ground. Breathe in sunlight through the top of your head, through your whole body and then out through the soles of your feet. Feel the golden flow of power moving through your body and into Gaia.
- Do this for at least five minutes.

Assertiveness

Assertiveness means being able to represent and advocate on behalf of yourself.

We can learn and cultivate assertive behaviour – our Lioness, Warrioress, Huntress and Athena are all good mentors for us in relation to this.

Assertive behaviour includes:

- Being able to discuss things that are bothering you

- Expressing your needs and emotions

- Making requests

- Being honest when you express

- Confidently and clearly expressing your own views and ideas

- Contributing

- Not fawning when someone strongly expresses an opinion different than your own

- Being able to say no

- Being able to firmly set boundaries

- Owning your voice and views with 'I'

- Starting and ending dialogue with others

All whilst being respectful of others and appreciating their viewpoint, even if it is different from your own.

Assertive women are Sacred Women. They self-advocate, self-lead, are emotionally resilient and bounce back from setbacks. They have willpower, and they set and follow their own intentions in a disciplined way.

Assess the assertiveness of your communication.

Do you actively listen?

Do you confidently express?

Do you make requests clearly – when it needs to happen, using I statements, making eye contact, etc.?

Do you express what the boundaries, expectations and consequences are?

If not – why?

Techniques to Try:

Lioness Mirror Work

Look in the mirror. Imagine your face is that of a Lioness. How would she express herself?

Warrioress Woman Stances: Channel Athena into your Body

Take up the two 'warrioress woman' postures daily.

Assertiveness Stance: Stand up straight. Put your hands on your hips. Breathe into your hips. Feel your feet on the ground. Breath power into your body.

Power Stance*: Stand up straight. Put your hands by the side of your body. Pull back your shoulders and allow chest to puff out. This is you owning and taking up space. You can also practise crossing your arms at your wrists in front of you to create a boundary and defence of your heart.

Bow and Arrow Huntress Yoga Pose: The ARROW of WILL

Imagine a goal you would like to achieve. Draw back your bow and fiery arrow of WILL. Take aim for the goal and let your bow and arrow soar and hit the centre of the goal, activating a catalysing explosion of manifesting, using this yoga pose.

AFFIRMATION and SYMBOL RITUAL

FOR MAGICAL INTENTION SETTING WITH THE FULL MOON

Developing SELF-EXPRESSION, LIGHT FEMININE MAGIC & WORTH.

MANIFESTING through THE IMPLEMENTATION OF PERSONAL WILL, THE MIND'S INTENTION & CONSCIOUSNESS.

At the festival of Litha, we connect with our HUNTRESS. We realise the POWER of the MIND and CONSCIOUS INTENT and then take clearly defined ACTIONS. We are a commanding consciousness, our own authority, as mighty, formidable cocreators with the Full Moon and Sun. The solar plexus is a portal of strength, resilience, and courage in the body, from which we can take decisive action.

Consciously training the mind to work for us is magical. We can use ritual and affirmation to do this and to support us to hunt and kill, to slay that which blocks us manifesting, through our personal and directive willpower and clarity of intention. Keeping our eyes, mind, and actions on the prize. Once we have visioned and checked that our personal will is in alignment with Divine and know our worthiness, we fuel manifestation through ovulation and harvest in the energy of Full Moon energy, giving thanks as our dreams birth into form.

Claiming growth through intention as the Solar Feminine and lioness is a radical act. The body can feel fear during the process so regulating and caring for your nervous system is essential as you assert yourself.

Going forward throughout the year, during every Full Moon and Ovulation, your Warrioress, Huntress and Lioness are dominant in your energy field and your sovereignty and Queendom are highly active. They want you to be infused with power, and be in the world as a wonder woman, with your mind working for you, to create abundance, worth and wealth, so you create, birth, and are seen as your unique self. Affirmation and symbol rituals anchor this into your magic toolbox, routine, and monthly planning at this time.

What you need:

- A citrine crystal (ideally a crystal point)
- Three other smaller crystals or stones
- Pen
- Paper to draw an upward triangle symbol
- Post-it notes
- Candle
- Sage stick for smudging
- Matches

The spell (your words) and the magical ritual:

- Burn some sage to smudge/energetically clear the area you are doing the magic spell in.

- Make sure you will be undisturbed.

- Take three deep breaths. Make sure you are 'in' your body.

- Ground and root yourself into Gaia's womb and through your crown connect with the energy of the Full Moon.

- Place your hand on your womb and forehead and think about your vision, your dream seed.

- Then create three self-worth or empowerment intentions of what you would like to birth into form that feel good to you and in your body. For example, to be able to stay strong and centred in conflict.

- Write them on a piece of paper and place them in the centre of the triangle.

- For each intention create an affirmation, a mantra, phrase, saying that you will repeat to yourself twice a day, morning and night, to train your brain that these intentions are possible.

- Write them on post-it notes.

- For example, if your intention is to stay strong during conflict, your affirmation on your post-it note could be, 'I am confident in my own viewpoint, regardless of external conditions.' 'I am' is the best way to start these intentions.

- Call forth Soul, the power of Goddess, Gaia, Sophia, the Full Moon, the Light and Solar Feminine, Athena and the power of your womb, heart, and mind and the Upper World and cosmic supporters.

- Place the three stones/crystals at each point of the triangle.

- Hold your citrine in your hand and starting at the top point, hold the crystal over the top point of the triangle and say, 'By the power of the full moon I am receiving...' and say your three intentions aloud. SPELL them with your voice. Self-express confidently.

- Hold the citrine over the bottom left point of the triangle and say, 'By the power of my mind and will, I am receiving...' and say your three intentions aloud.

- Hold the citrine over the bottom right point of the triangle and say, 'By the power of Goddess and Athena, I am receiving...' and say your three intentions aloud.

- Then place the citrine over the folded paper intentions in the centre and say, 'It is done' three times and, 'So it is' three times and then finish by saying, 'This is for the highest good of all.'

- Take your post-it notes and place them on a mirror in your bedroom. Place the mirror by your bed. Every day for the next month – as soon as you wake up and before you go to sleep – look at lioness self in the mirror and say the three affirmations aloud.

In your day-to-day life, take daily actions to support your intentions to birth into form. Take aim, hunt, and slay. Bounce back from setbacks. Implement, organise, and follow your inner compass.

Leave the grid in place for the full lunation – full moon to full moon. Then take it apart in reverse order, stone by stone, with gratitude, and thanking the moon, your mind and willpower, Goddess, and Athena.

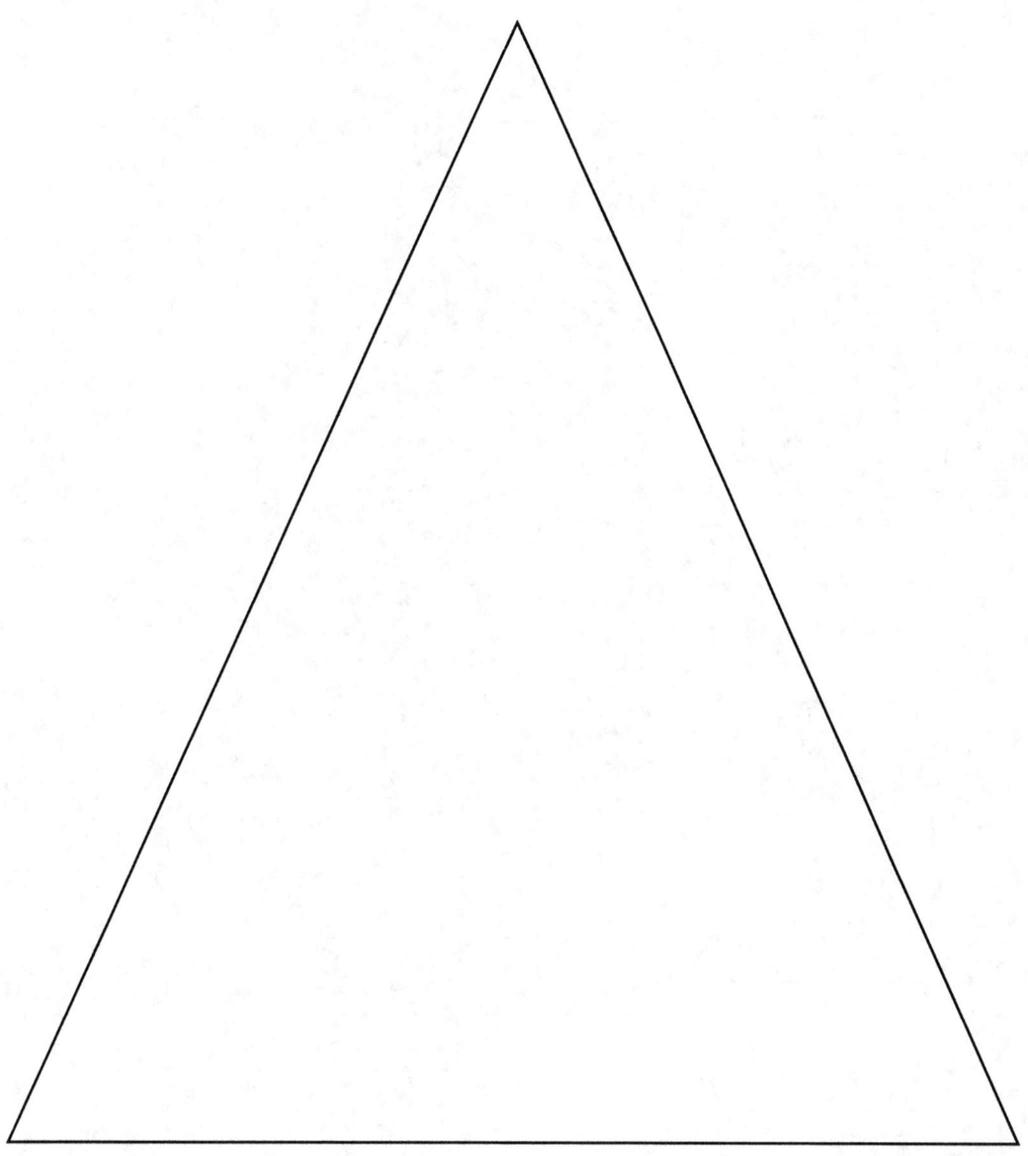

Painting by Kat Shaw

Introduction to Green Module

KEY CONCEPTS TO INTEGRATE:

NURTURER: one who nourishes, cherishes, cares, and sustains.

RELEASE: let go, liberate, free.

COLLECTIVE: shared.

COMMUNITY: group.

ENVIRONMENT: nature, ecosystem, earth.

SISTERHOOD: women group bond.

MINDFULNESS: awareness in the present moment.

ABUNDANCE: plenty, wealth, richness.

SELF-LOVE: loving oneself, caring for your own well-being.

SELF-ACCEPTANCE: accepting oneself, without judgement.

SELF-COMPASSION: kindness, non-judgement and understanding for oneself when
suffering.

ONENESS: unified, whole.

LOVE: deep affection, tenderness, feelings, devotion.

SACRED HEART: our mystical, devotional, spiritual heart.

NARRATIVE: story.

MADONNA-WHORE SPLIT: A Freudian-identified patriarchal phenomenon where men are
unable to respect and love the women they sexually desire: 'the whore,' and conversely are
unable to sexually desire those women they respect and love, 'the madonna.' An insidious
paradigm is still active today within society, advertising, collective opinion, and the psyche.

Month: August

Season: Late Summer

Festival: Lammas

Direction: South-West

Element: Fire

Goddess archetype: NURTURER – Goddess Mary Magdalene

Symbol: Infinity sign

Animal: Deer

Moon: Waning Gibbous

Menstrual: Post-ovulation

Body area: Breasts and lungs

Chakra: Heart

Crystal: Rose quartz (love, harmony, self-love, peace, healing, forgiveness, trust)

Oil: Rose (stress relief, harmony, love, care, comfort, soothing)

In this module, you will connect with your NURTURER and your HEART, your BREASTS and LUNGS, the home of LOVE in your body. This is the area from which you RELEASE grief and experience deep connection with the ENVIRONMENT and the COLLECTIVE. The frequency of your Nurturer, aided by the gentleness of your Deer and allyship of Mary Magdalene, also holds the coding of SELF-LOVE, SELF-ACCEPTANCE and SELF-COMPASSION. In this module you are initiated into Sacred Woman SISTERHOOD and global COMMUNITY, assisted by the energetics of relaxation post-ovulation and full moon and ABUNDANCE. At Lammas you deepen into relationship with Gaia and environmental awareness, grateful for the bounty that the earth gifts us at this first harvest festival.

Connection to your own and the collective NARRATIVE are integral to this module. Through MINDFULNESS and self-reflection, you explore alternative personal stories and their endings, empowering yourself, redefining who and how you are in the world. In doing so you liberate your ancestral lines, Sisterhood and the collective, and begin to see you, feel, and know ONENESS and that Goddess is within everything – anger and compassion, passion and innocence, body and mind, lover, and nurturer.

During this module you will explore trauma and hurt lovingly and embrace your inner child, caring for her and self-parenting all parts of SELF. The element of fire supports the warming to, acceptance and love of shadow aspects. In addition, as you become ever more conscious of ONENESS, you begin to anchor love, compassion and understanding into your Sacred Womanhood incarnation through the activation of your SACRED HEART.

The Goddess Archetype for the Green Module

NURTURER – Goddess Mary Magdalene

Mary Magdalene, reclaimed from the patriarchal biblical distortion of 'prostitute,' is the High Priestess who was the companion, and indeed some argue wife, equal and lover of Jesus. She was the nurturer of his body, with him at his crucifixion and first witness to the empty tomb and the 'resurrection.' She is the one who told her community stories of rebirth, rising and the preciousness of embodiment. She teaches us about love, our physical and sacred heart, and the liberation of the body and sexuality from shame. She shows us that to feel deeply – to experience emotional depth – is not a mental illness, but a vital part of Sacred Womanhood.

Legends around Mary Magdalene include the story that her body is the Holy Grail, as lover of Jesus and mother and nurturer of their children. She is an amazing mentor, showing us that we can be both sexual and nurturing, with fiery eroticism and gentle space-holding compassion. She supports us to 'exorcise' from our minds the patriarchal madonna-whore split and to recover oneness as a woman, of mind and body – of thought and feeling and the sacredness of all emotions, including anger. She reminds us again that the body IS Goddess.

She shows that we can author our own life – *we* are in charge of the narrative.

Take a moment to reflect on this and your relationship with the madonna-whore (mother-lover, good-bad girl, spiritual-sexual) split.

- *What does your mind say about it?*
- *What do you feel in your body?*
- *What would it take for you to feel integrated and whole?*

Welcome to August. The season of Green. The Earth is abundant, full, and plentiful. Lifeforce is languid, oozing, and sensual. Late summer is here. The growth is done and it's time to celebrate the earth's bounty, the nurturance we have received through the glory of Gaiaspace-holding and our own body. We are ready to rest in the woozy warmth of a more tempered pace and heat of the sun. We are prepared to review and celebrate our accomplishments as we gather in the first grain crops and produce.

The festival of Lammas (Loaf Mass, the feast of bread) falls on the wheel of the year halfway between Litha, the Summer Solstice and Mabon, the Autumn Equinox. The calendared date for the festival is August 1st or 2nd. This is the first harvest festival of the year. At this festival we experience maturity, the joy of community, and we celebrate collaboration and union. It is a pause, a time to congratulate and express gratitude to our body, our family and friends, partners, community, and the earth. It reminds us of interdependence, giving and receiving, and the need to support and be harmonious.

We can slow down into flow as preparation for the winter months complete, the food is gathered in, and the element of water enters our energy field. Our connection to Goddess and our interdependence on her body for our life is at its peak. Goddess has conceived, gestated, and birthed life. Now she will regenerate. It is time for her and us to journey inward again. Motherhood and nurturance are celebrated fully at this festival as the Crone, the dark, calls us more insistently. The spring and summer are exhausted. We have completed the outer action. At Lammas we pause, say thank you and release, let go. Like the earth, we are ready to rest, integrate and renew.

Corn Mother was the primary focus for the traditional celebrations at Lammas.

Breadmaking, crop circles, grass, corn, and herb crowns were part of the festivities. The last sheaf of corn was cut at Harvest Full Moon and made into a corn dolly and hung above the home mantlepiece during autumn and winter in honour of Goddess, a visual reminder that spring will return and as a promise of a good harvest the following year. On Lammas Eve, fires would once more be lit in thanks to the sun, which is now waning. The community would join to celebrate their mutual support for one another, eating, drinking, and dancing. On the fire there would be a large cooking cauldron, symbol of regeneration and the transformative union of fire – sun – day – light – life and water – moon – night – dark – death. There were also village markets and swapping of harvest produce as the community came together as one. Ego and individuality had no place at this festival.

At Lammas we ask ourselves: *What blocks do I need to clear out of my mind, body, energy, environment, and relationships to create space for more connection and trust in Sisterhood? What do I need less of?* Conversely, we ask ourselves: *What do I need to invite into my mind, body, energy, environment, and relationships? What do I need more of? What needs to happen for me to reclaim my trust in community?*

We have the opportunity to enquire… *What do I want the story of my life to be? Which narratives can I release to the composting process and which seed do I want to keep for planting?*

Our Doe is one of the oldest symbols of the magic. It offers us the energy of grace, gentleness, intuition, and sensitivity. It reminds us we can be compassionate and kind when dealing with challenges and that we can navigate these situations and obstacles with grace and ease. The doe is a mystical and often shy creature, who offers us a doorway into our inner child. Herds of doe stick together to ensure safety and plentiful food. They connect and create together, and they have collective power. They tread gently on their environment; they are not destructive. In the same way – at Lammas and during the Waning Gibbous phase of the lunar cycle – we connect and lean into companionship and collaboration for the greatest good of community and creativity, open to change if need be. This is a phase of the menstrual cycle, just after ovulation, when we feel a softening, alongside connection through oestrogen for bonding, rather than individual frenzied gain.

The ancient symbol of the infinity sign is a representation of completeness. Its origin was in the world of Arabic mathematics and numerals. It is a symbol of wholeness, infinity itself, endlessness – and is coded with concepts such equality, balance and the union of yang and yin, male, and female, right and left, sun and moon – alongside union sexually (the Hieros m), the sacred marriage, which it was thought Mary Magdalene and Jesus entered into) two becoming one. It is the action made during handfasting, the ancient pagan marriage ritual, common at Lammas.

At this time of year, it is a good to be outside to soak up the final rays of the sun, filling yourself up with light and radiance (and vitamin D!) in preparation for the introspective internal season of late autumn and winter. Celebrate what you are reaping now, based on the seeds sown in the spring. Reward and praise yourself. If there were any dream seeds you planted that did not grow mindfully, reflect on why you think that was with radical self-acceptance and love. Ensure your inner child is loved – and that there is no disappointment or shame with self, only understanding. This is a time to reflect on learnings and let go, release, empty out, and ready for visioning.

Most of all, we come into loving nurturance with self and other this month. It's about cultivating oneness with self and community.

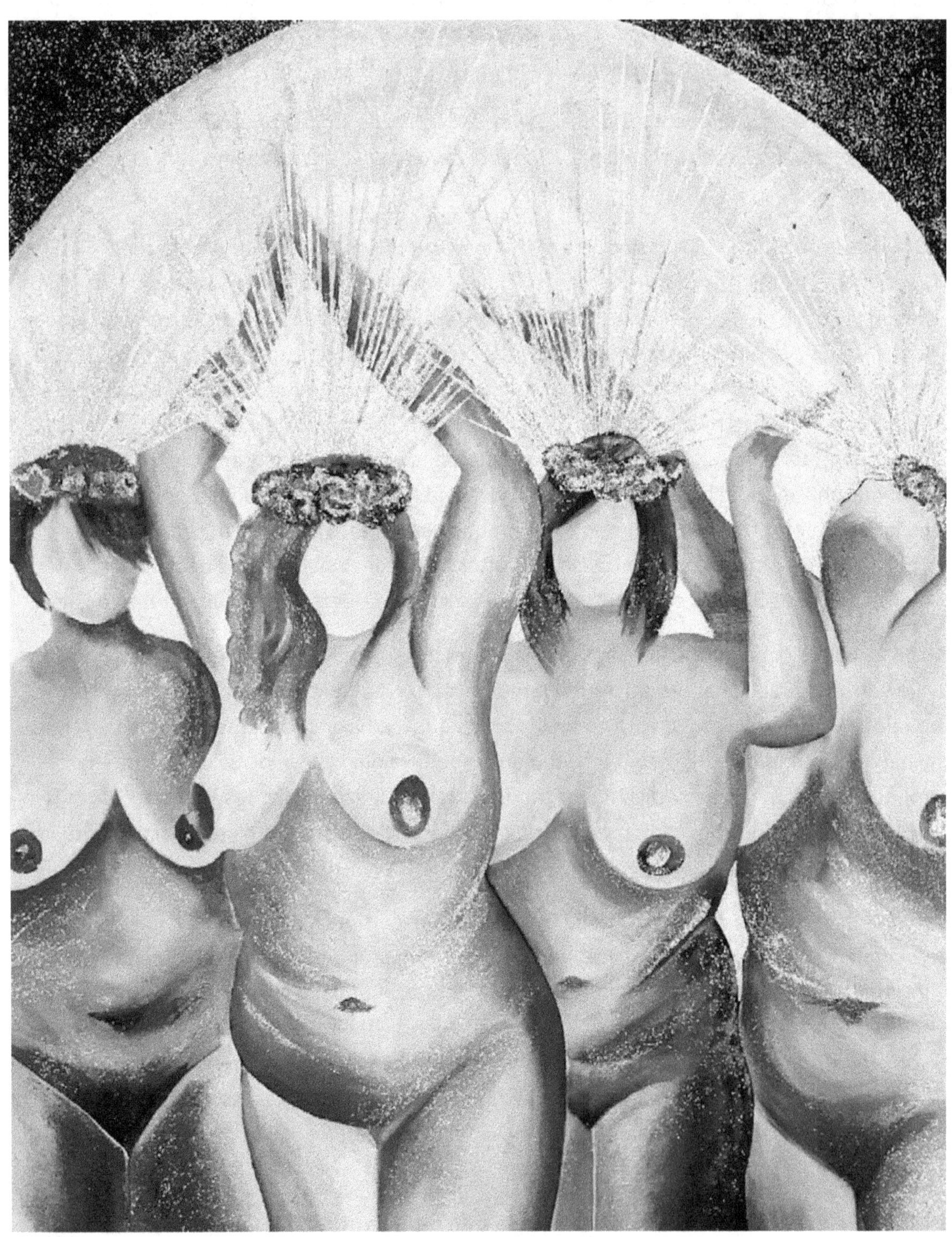

Art by Kat Shaw

Your Body, Nervous System, and Energy in August

August is the time to connect and feel cherished and nourished, so that you are sustained throughout the autumn and winter. To feel and unite with love and nourishment at this time through radical self-acceptance and self-compassion. It is time to come into relationship with your heart chakra (Anahata, which translates as unhurt) and start to calm the sympathetic nervous system through self-love and connection to self, Sisterhood, and community. In this module you are also going to become aware of (and develop a relationship with) your breasts and lungs.

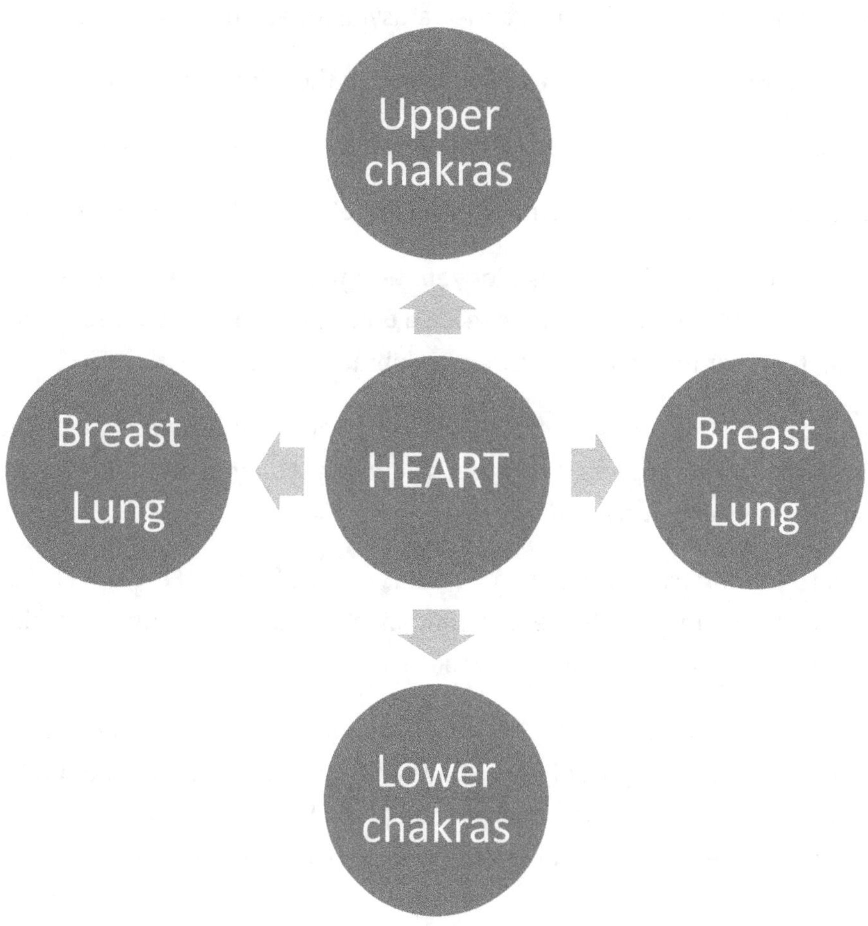

BODY

- Go outside for at least 1 hour each day.

- Continue to drink plenty of fluids but also introduce more greens into your diet this month. Kale, lettuce, and beans are good examples.

- Do breathwork exercises from the Rainbow Diamond Centre module as active meditations and as a support for well-being through the conscious release of held emotions. Remember emotions are meant to move through us – they are energy-in-motion. Breathe in these ways for at least three minutes each day,

Left Nostril Breathing – to calm us – engage the parasympathetic nervous system.

Close off the right nostril and breathe in and out through the left nostril only.

6-6-6 Breath – to create balance – the expel that which is held in your lungs and body.

Breathe in for count of 6. Hold the breath for the count of 6. Exhale for the count of 6.

- Make a music playlist of love songs for your best friends, and your Sisters. Share it with them individually, sending them each a unique message of appreciation and love. Join together for a dance party and celebrate each other.

- Connect to your community. Research a cause, a topic you feel passionate about. Find a charity which supports this cause in your local community. Volunteer your time and skills in some way to them.

- Connect to your breasts – get to know what is normal for you. Feel and check them twice a week for a month. Notice how they change with your menstrual cycle or the lunar cycle. Know what is normal for you.

- Become intimate with your BREASTS and LUNGS. It is empowering and useful to use a mirror to look at every part of your body and to touch all parts of your body. Remember: It is totally normal for any area of your body to have hair on it, including your breasts. Note also: A lot of pleasure is to be had from touching our breasts.

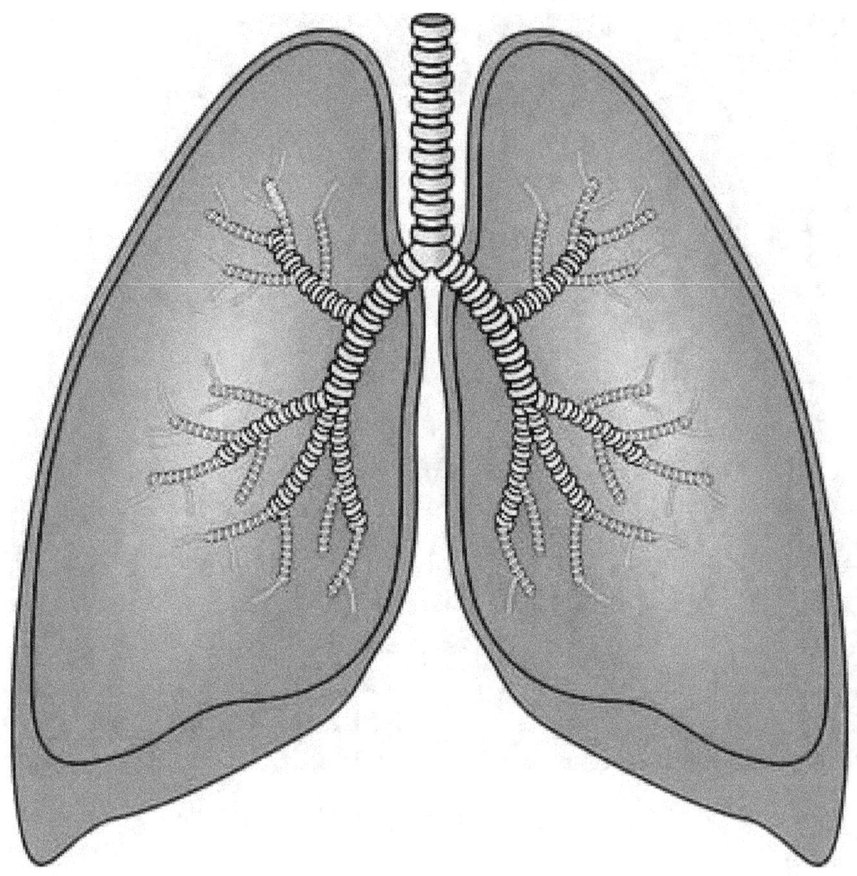

Clavicle (collarbone): Top part of breast tissue.

Chest muscles: Support arm movement.

Sternum: Breastbone.

Ribs: Bone encasement of lungs.

Lungs: Organs on left and right side of chest which fill and empty with inhaled and exhaled air through the trachea (windpipe) and bronchi. Oxygenate the blood on inhale and remove carbon dioxide on exhale.

Axillary lymph nodes under armpits: Filter lymph fluid from the breasts and support the body to fight infection.

Mammary glands – produce milk during pregnancy and breastfeeding

Ducts – carry milk during breastfeeding from mammary glands

Fatty tissue – lifts areas around mammary glands and ducts

Fibrous tissue – supports firmness of breasts

Nipple – exit area for milk during breastfeeding

Areola – dark area of skin around the nipple

NERVOUS SYSTEM

- Connect to your breasts, lungs, and heart. Send them mindful presence, radical acceptance, gratitude, and love. Do this every bedtime for a month.

Once you are settled into bed, consciously feel your back against the mattress. Breathe in deeply to the front of the body then breathe out deeply through the back of the body into the mattress. Do this for a couple of minutes.

Fill your hands with presence, gratitude, and love.

Place your hands lovingly on your breasts and connect with the treasure chest of organs in your body, the breasts, lungs, and ribcage.

Allow this space in your body to rise and fall at its own pace. Do not force it. Simply give the body mindful presence, radial acceptance, gratitude, and love.

On every exhale say silently in your mind – THANK YOU.

ENERGY: Heart Chakra

Dominant 22–28 years.

The green wheel and energy vortex located in the centre of the breasts and rib cage. Visualising this supports the energy there to clear and enhance.

Placing your hands on your womb and repeating the mantra, 'I love. I accept. I care. I forgive. I trust. I give. I receive.' will also support this chakra to strengthen.

Sitting up and drawing the shape of the infinity sign across your breasts and chest – whilst breathing in and out deeply from front and back of the chest – will also support the body to connect more powerfully to oneness and the mysteries and power of your sacred heart.

When in balance, this chakra offers us harmony, connectivity, self-love, compassion, empathy, acceptance, forgiveness, peace, awareness, and oneness.

When out of balance, we may experience hard-heartedness, loneliness, insecurity, inability to give and receive love, feeling shut down, resentfulness and bitterness, co-dependency, jealousy, respiratory and heart-related issues.

The heart chakra teaches us that our body is the portal of LOVE. We are the manifestation of Love. The heart chakra anchors the sacred heart into human form and shows us the vital importance of self-care and self-love, self-acceptance for care, love, and acceptance of others. It teaches us to fill ourselves up first, to give from abundance, an over-spilling cup.

Heart opening exercise for oneness.

Stand up.

Place a grounding cord into Gaia.

Place your hands in the centre of your chest in prayer position.

Inhale.

Exhale… opening out your arms, feeling and seeing your inner child running towards you.

Inhale.

Exhale and close your arms around your inner child, giving her a huge hug.

Repeat five times.

- Then do the same for those you love
- Then for your friends and community
- Then for all of humanity
- Then for the earth

Embrace it all. Feel in your heart how everything is connected.

GROUND

Feel at One with the Earth.

Lie flat, face down on the ground.

Feel your breasts against the body of Gaia.

Inhale into the centre of the chest. As you exhale, imagine a root coming from the centre of the rib cage, the heart chakra, through your body, out into the earth, and moving through all the layers of soil, deeper and deeper into Gaia until you feel your heart cord connect to the heartbeat of the earth.

Inhale the heartbeat and the generosity and abundant heart energy of the earth into your heart chakra and exhale, releasing self-criticism, judgement, grief, and harshness.

Feel the softening and filling up.

Do this for at least five minutes.

Author the narrative of your Sacred Womanhood from your Sacred Heart

Release and Renewal

Write your Sacred Woman Story

This activity supports you to consciously navigate change. To vision from your Sacred Heart your part in the collective and growth of Sacred Womanhood and what your story is as a Sacred Woman.

The stories we tell carry an energy, they dream weave, they are the way we cast spells, we spell out the reality we want to live in.

We make our life story work for us, use the eros of imagination to support easeful and graceful change for ourselves, future and past generations and the collective.

Stories are that powerful!

Release

It may be that you already know the narratives, the stories you want to release. The page of the book of your life that you want to rip out and burn. The paragraph you want to draw a line under.

Here is a ritual to help you with this:

- Get a piece of paper and write a list of people, places, thoughts, behaviours, memories, actions you would like to release from your life story.

- Then write a list of thoughts, opinions, behaviours, views of womanhood, you would like to release from your life story. They can be personal to you or collective conditioning. For example, domestic abuse, sexual assault, unequal pay, objectification, good girl-bad girl split.

- Then write a list of all the ways the earth is being destroyed and harmed. The things you would like to stop. For example, deforestation, climate change.

- Then take the paper and burn it. As you burn it say, 'By the power of my mind, body and heart, and by the power of Goddess and Sacred Womanhood, I release this from my own life and energy field, from the collective and from Gaia.' Then say, 'So it is' three times, and finish by saying, 'This is for the highest good of all.'

Offer the ashes to the earth and wash your hands.

Connect to your Sacred Heart

Draw your physical and sacred heart below. *What is the difference?*

Put your hand on your sacred heart – in your heart chakra – and ask it to show you what you are passionate about and devoted to.

You may hear, see, feel, or just 'know' the answer.

Write it down here.

Write down three words/phrases/sentences for each of the following which describe your visions of –

Self-love:

Self-compassion:

Self-acceptance:

Embodiment:

Relationship:

Intimacy:

Community:

Sisterhood:

Friendship:

Home:

Earth:

Hobbies:

Life Purpose:

Finances:

Sacred Womanhood:

Goddess:

Career:

Education/Learning:

Health:

Society:

Culture:

Childhood:

Write down three hopes and dreams you have for –

Your Mind:

Your Body:

Your Life:

And then three dreams you have for future generations of womanhood:

And three hopes you have for society:

And finally, three hopes you have for the earth:

Use everything you wrote down (and anything else you'd like to add) to create the **new story of your life**. When you have finished, light a candle, and read it aloud to Goddess and to your body, mind and heart.

Finish by saying, 'I pledge to embody this now. And so it is. And so it is. And so it is. For the highest good of all'

NURTURING RITUAL and MAGIC FOR SELF-RECLAMATION

BREAST MASSAGE AND INNOCENT EROTIC SENSUALITY

Recovering the breasts from the 'male gaze,' pornography and sexualisation.

At the festival of Lammas, we connect to the NURTURER. We realise that we are MORE THAN objectification and that our bodies, especially the nourishment offered by our breasts, are not a resource for others, unless we choose to offer them as so. Our breasts have been (at least to some extent) pornographically conditioned by a 'male gaze' (i.e., sexualised subjects and objects for sexual arousal, viewed by society through the lens of male, heterosexual pleasure) and unfortunately, we have internalised this. In addition, the breasts, their size, purpose, visibility, clothes on them or otherwise are an aspect of the madonna-whore complex.

Touching our breasts consciously and exploring them innocently, non-sexually, and for our self, our curiosity, and the delight of touching our own skin (allowing for any pleasure to arise and enjoying it if it does) can be a new ritual for us – and through touch, we both activate and strengthen our magic and the power of Goddess, that we are. Nurturing our breasts for our OWN sake, reclaiming our breasts to be for us whatever we want them to be is a revolutionary and political act.

The body can feel fear during the process – and the mind may have a lot to say, so go slowly and mindfully, radically accept yourself, listen to and LOVE and care for all aspects of Self.

As you do this for yourself you liberate the Sisterhood and collective to do the same.

Going forward throughout the year every Waning Gibbous Moon, and/or just after ovulation, your Nurturer is predominant in your energy field, and you are softening into a compassionate, self-soothing, loving flow. She wants you to be infused with love and oneness! To feel whole and holy, complete and in union. That nurturer and lover, innocence, and eroticism, can always coexist. That you can be all you want to be moment-to-moment. Nurturing breast massage is a ritual to anchor into your magic toolbox, routine, and monthly planning at this time.

What you need:

- A room where you will be undisturbed and can look out onto a garden or green space. If this is not possible, then select a room where you will be undisturbed and can look at a vase of fresh flowers or a plan.
- Your favourite essential oils, ideally rose oil diluted with a carrier oil of your choice or a plain moisturiser.
- Your rose quartz crystal.
- A bowl of warm water.
- Clean towel.
- A candle.
- Sage stick for smudging.
- Matches.
- Glue.
- Notebook.
- Pen.

Creating your ritual space:

- Light your candle.
- Burn some sage to smudge/energetically clear the area you are creating the wand in.
- Make sure you will be undisturbed.

The ritual itself:

- Take three deep breaths. Make sure you are 'in' your body.

- Ground and root yourself into Gaia's womb and connect with the greenness, the wonder of the environment, Gaia's body, her creation – the outdoor space, the flowers, the plant.

- Place your hands, your fingertips, on sternum. Pause and notice the feelings, thoughts and sensations that arise. Infuse your fingertips with the touch of pure innocence, curiosity, awe, and wonder. And anything else you choose.

- Look again at Gaia's body, the flowers, the plant. Imagine your body is her. Imagine how innocently you might touch grass or joyfully look at a beautiful flower. Imagine your breasts are as precious and as beautiful as that.

- Then speak out loud these three intentions for this nurturing ritual:

  - ➢ To reclaim the innocence of my breasts.

  - ➢ To cut the cords with the male and pornographic gaze on my breasts.

  - ➢ To recover my breasts as part of my body and myself as their gatekeeper.

- Call forth the power of Goddess, Mary Magdalene, Earth, Air, Fire, Water, Gaia and the power of your womb, heart, and mind.

- Ask Mary Magdalene to guide you.

- Place your rose quartz into the bowl of warm water to cleanse and warm up.

- Take some of the rose oil mixed with the carrier oil or moisturiser in your hands and gently stroke and touch every part of your chest and breasts.

- As you do so, say out loud 'I see you,' 'I reclaim your innocence,' 'I love you,' 'I appreciate you.'

- Go slowly, pause if you need to. Less is more. Stop when you feel complete. You can always do this again.

- Activate your innocent erotic sensuality with the rose quartz.

- Take the rose quartz out of the warm water and hold it at the centre of your heart chakra – in between the breasts. Look out at Gaia and say out loud, 'With the graceful ease of my Doe and through my oneness with the Earth and all women, I activate this crystal with the innocence of every part of my body and the innocence of my erotic sensuality.'

- Hold your crystal over your left breast and say, 'By the power of the Rose I reclaim the innocence of my breasts, I cut the cords with the male and pornographic gaze on my breasts, I recover my breasts as part of my body and myself as their gatekeeper.'

- Hold your crystal over your right breast and say, 'By the power of Mary Magdalene I reclaim the innocence of my breasts, I cut the cords with the male and pornographic gaze on my breasts. I recover my breasts as part of my body and myself as their gatekeeper.'

- Hold your crystal in the centre of your breasts, at your heart chakra and say, 'By the power of Goddess and Sacred Womanhood I reclaim the innocence of my breasts, I cut the cords with the male and pornographic gaze on my breasts, I recover my breasts as part of my body and myself as their gatekeeper.'

- Then say, 'It is done' three times and, 'So it is' three times. and then finish by saying, 'This is for the highest good of all.'

Take three deep inhales and exhales.

When you feel complete, thank Gaia and Mary Magdalene for their love and companionship and mentorships. Perhaps journal about your experience.

If you feel aroused self-pleasure yourself, holding the intention of reclaiming your body and touch for yourself, to fill yourself up.

Store your oils and crystal in your cloth magical tool kit bag.

Painting by Kat Shaw

Introduction to Blue Module

KEY CONCEPTS TO INTEGRATE:

RELATIONSHIPS: connection between two or more people or things.

COMMUNICATION: exchanging (sending or receiving) information.

NEEDS: our requirements.

TRUTH: that which is our own known reality.

VOICE: vocal expression of our truth.

REFLECTION: taking time to consider and discern.

LIFE AUDIT: assessment of our life.

AUTHENTICITY: genuine, unique, real.

BOUNDARIES: limit what is ok and not ok.

ABUSE: misuse, cruelty, violence, persistent maltreatment.

PATRIARCHY: societal systems and structures in which the masculine dominates the feminine and men hold 'power over' and dominance of women.

CORD CUTTING: unhooking self and severing energy cords from unhealthy and draining people, places, objects, behaviours, memories, relationships.

VULNERABILITY: willingness to be seen and express sensitivity.

Month: September

Season: Early Autumn

Festival: Mabon

Direction: West

Element: Water

Goddess archetype: WISE WOMAN – The Goddess Morrigan

Symbol: Athame (dagger)

Animal: Wolf

Moon: Last Quarter

Menstrual: Pre-menstrual

Body area: Throat

Chakra: Throat

Crystal: Lapis Lazuli (speak truth, effective communication, self-awareness, express emotions)

Oil: Peppermint (self-expression, clarity of communication)

In this module you will connect with your WISE WOMAN and your THROAT AND VOICE, home of TRUTH in your body. This is the area from which you use your voice and Athame to CORD CUT and set BOUNDARIES – and to express your NEEDS, ask for help and embrace your VULNERABILITY. Your Wise Woman also holds the frequency of AUTHENTICITY, honest self-expression, within the container of self-protection through BOUNDARIES, which your Wolf and The Morrigan help you navigate and set. In this module you are initiated into soulful VOICE, your NEEDS and affirming RELATIONSHIPS. You deepen in relationship with your internal wisdom, guidance, and soul. And re-engage in REFLECTION and take another look at the assessment activity, the LIFE AUDIT you did earlier in the year.

Connection to your own VOICE and TRUTH are integral to this module. Through sounding and speaking we refine our COMMUNICATION skills and empower ourselves, ensuring our needs are met. We consider healthy relationships and educate ourselves about ABUSE. Goddess ensures that the vulnerable are protected. She is an activist against violence and power-over dynamics.

In this module you will learn CORD CUTTING techniques. The element of water supports flow of change and cleansing process as you assess, release, and refocus before the winter.

During this module you become ever more conscious of dismantling PATRIARCHY and power over dynamics that perpetuate harm for you, other humans, and the earth. As Goddess rises, shared power becomes the norm – a culture where everyone can live and speak from their own truth.

WISE WOMAN – The Morrigan

The Morrigan is an Irish Goddess in origin. She is the Great Queen of the warrior cry, prophetess of fate and war, and the Goddess of bravery, earth, and our own truth. She manifests in different ways and is a true shape shifter, adaptable and ever-changing. Her forms include washer woman on the battlefield, a raven, and a wolf. She has many names and has been linked energetically to Kali and in the Arthurian legends is thought to be Morgan le Fay of the Isle of Avalon.

She is often depicted as an oracle – speaking, foretelling, or singing – sharing her powerful inner knowing. Her mentorship strengthens our voice, ability to communicate effectively and set appropriate boundaries. She protects heroines who battle against injustice and abuse.

Legends of her hunger for embodiment (she is known for her gusty libido, consensually enjoying sex with a god) will support us as we own our own erotic desires, including sexual ones, and express our needs clearly and without shame. The Morrigan lived entirely in her authenticity – non-conformist, raw and unconstrained. She knows how to work with energy, wield a sword of light and do battle with inauthenticity – slaying that which no longer serves us or the greatest good.

As the gatekeeper of death, she shows that we can end old ways of being, speaking, acting – swiftly and without drama – and reclaim our full embodiment.

Take a moment to reflect on this and your relationship with death.

How do you feel about death?

What does your mind say about it?

What is your relationship with your voice, your truth and setting boundaries?

Welcome to September. The season of Blue. The Earth is offering us the energy of harvest and thanksgiving. Lifeforce is integrated, as we, Gaia, and the Cosmos come into balance and harmony. Day and Night are again in perfect equilibrium. This is a time of reflection and choice. Change is coming. The sap of the trees starts moving down, withdrawing, and withering, and browning of plants becomes visible and we must quickly gather in the fruits and store them for the winter. There is less heat in the sun's rays. Light and dark, day and night, hot and cold, swap places. As the season of autumn fully takes hold and we transition into the darkest half of the year and know, in our mind, bodies and energy that winter is coming.

The festival of Mabon (the Autumn Equinox) is halfway between Lammas and Samhain on the Wheel of the Year and the calendar date is September 20th-23rd. This is the time of year to tidy and complete outdoor jobs and external projects. Reap what you have sown – prune, sweep and clear the path for the new internal and quiet phase. It is a good time to have one final hurrah – gathering with friends and family, perhaps outside for the final time – to give thanks to the Earth and all that she has provided for us and to celebrate our own external achievements. We also reflect on what we can give back, how we can reciprocate with those who have supported us.

As at Ostara, we are reminded again at this Equinox that Goddess encompasses everything; life and death, flourishing and rotting, flesh and spirit, doing and being, masculine and feminine, light and dark. We are reminded that the only certainty is change and that cycles never cease. Mabon signals the onset of the rest and renewal phase – time for internal transformation, to tune into our own truth, and intuition, to plan and incubate and resting into faith and trust that the dream seeds we place in the earth now will grow anew, stronger, and more resilient in the spring.

We call again on the dragon energy of Gaia, her fire, erotic, red lifeforce – and light the flames within us, activate our womb and voice, so we can express our needs and say no, moving through the unconscious and liminal realms, before the Earth calls it back for her own regeneration and recuperation. We fill up with gratitude and surrender willingly to our own internal guidance, direction, and compass. At Mabon we take our sword and draw a line in the sand, a boundary, and sign of completion of what has been. This is the pause between breaths, the space between stories, the boundary between what is known and seen – and what is unknown and unseen. We then clear the slate ready to receive the visions of our next incarnation of self.

Lighting bonfires and burning scarecrows represent the dying light and death of the Sun God and our ego death. Walking labyrinths represent the walking inwards at Mabon and strong fire drumming is about sounding a boundary to protect against fear as we begin the path of walking the shadow.

We can slow down into flow even further than at Lammas. Preparations for the winter months are now fully completed, the food is gathered in, and the element of water flows completely in our energy field. Celebration of abundance and space clearing are the primary focus for the traditional celebrations at Mabon. Harvest decorations, tables, altars, shrines, and baskets (showcasing the wide array of leaves, berries and produce), harvest suppers, tree planting, and bulb planting are popular activities of this festival. Taking time to go outside and thank a tree by hugging it is a lovely way to commune with Gaia and her dragon energy before the retreat inwards and downwards begins. Finishing garden projects, splitting herb plants, collecting seeds for spring, harvesting herbs, as well as cleaning out the home, decluttering, cleaning, and sage smudging, supporting cord cutting and energy cleansing prepares for the wheel of the year to turn.

Herb storage, bundle and smudge-making are also activities commonly practised at Mabon. They support health, as well as journeying, clearing the voice for spellcasting, intention setting, and cord cutting. Common herbs harvested at this time of year are fennel and hops. Hawthorn berries are also a supporting heart plant ally, keeping our hearts bright during the winter months.

Sound is a huge aspect of this festival. Harmonising, humming, drumming all support the activation of the power of our own voice and truth. Harvest barn, circle dancing, and dragon dancing are also all common activities. The focus for these is weaving balance.

Finally, assessment, letting go, and releasing for balance is also a practised ritual and ceremony at Mabon. Cord cutting, writing things down and burning them, clearing out clutter, and setting new intentions all encourage space clearing.

At this time, we ask ourselves: *What blocks do I need to clear out of my mind, body, energy, environment, and relationships to create space for more authentic relationships and to empower my truthful voice? What do I need less of?* Conversely, we ask ourselves: *What do I need to invite into my mind, body, energy, environment, and relationships? What do I need more of? What needs to happen for me to reclaim my boundaries and authenticity?*

We consider, *what do I want my relationships to be like? Which cords need to be cut?*

Our Wolf connects us – both to community and our own individual path. She offers us the energy of wildness and our raw, authentic, truth. She reminds us that we are wise and powerful and have an inner-knowing which can be our compass. In addition, wolf supports us to protect and set boundaries according to our instinct. If threatened or betrayed by others, the wolf teaches us to walk away and seek out a non-abusive, life-affirming pack instead. Our wolf offers us our howl, the lifegiving voice and call to devotion to the supportive pack.

The Athame is the symbol for this module. The Athame is a knife or dagger used ceremonially by our wise woman, it is a magical tool used for casting ceremonial space, circles, or symbols and for cord cutting. This will empower us to release ourselves from dysfunction and to cut the cords with that which no longer serves us.

The death process begins at Mabon and the Great Goddess Morrigan walks us into our shadowlands.

Your Body, Nervous System, and Energy in September

September is the month to authentically connect and relate – to your truth, yourself and to others in relationship. It is time to self-reflect again, assess and release. It is the stage to come into relationship with your throat chakra (Vishuddha, which means pure) to start to speak your truth, set boundaries and relate from the heart. In this module you are also going to become aware of and develop a relationship with your voice. It is the phase to feel protected and confident in both self-assertion and vulnerability, asking for your needs to be met and to express your emotions. Your voice and emotions and truth of your womb are inextricably linked energetically and physically as you will learn.

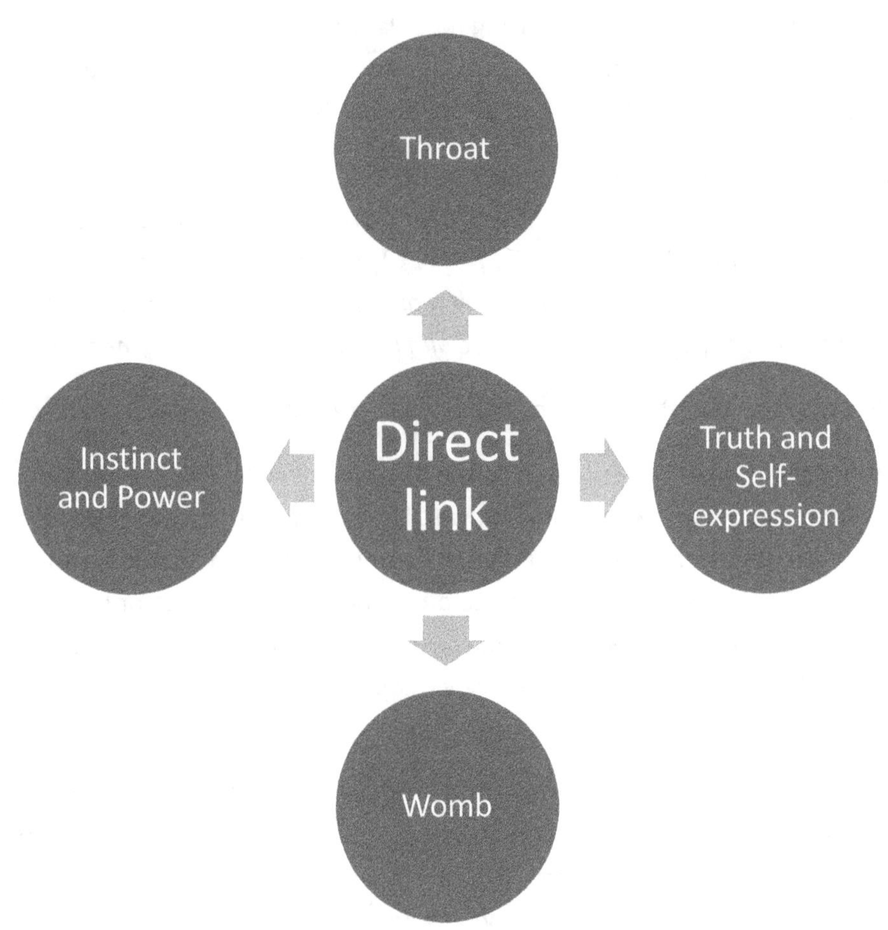

Throat
Instinct and Power
Direct link
Truth and Self-expression
Womb

BODY

- Go outside for at least 1 hour each day.

- Continue to drink plenty of fluids but also introduce darker foods – more berries such as blackberries and blueberries – into your diet. Add aubergine, nuts, and seeds too.

- Use Breathwork to clear the throat chakra and to clear the pathway from the womb to throat. Do this Wolf Breath for three minutes each day this month.

Wolf Breath

- ➢ Inhale through the nose.
- ➢ Open your mouth wide and stick out your tongue.
- ➢ Push out the exhaled breath with the sound of a loud howl or panting.

As you exhale, also feel your perineum drop to the chair or floor and allow the belly to stick out, loosening the abdomen muscles.

- Look on YouTube or Spotify for the 7-chakra vowel sounds and listen to them twice a week, joining in.

- Assess your body's reactions to social media. If you are connected to any pages and feeds to which your body reacts uncomfortably – consider unfollowing. Look at your own social media feeds. *Are you being truthful and authentic? How does your body react? Where can changes be made?* Consider following body-positive, female-positive, and inclusivity feeds that resonate with you.

- Connect to your physical voice – its tone, volume, clarity, and strength. *How does it feel to speak your name aloud? How does it feel to verbally express your needs?* Practice speaking in front of a mirror, answering these sentences daily:

  I am...

  I notice...

  I need...

  I feel...

  Thank you for hearing me.

- Get to know your womb-throat connection. When the pelvic floor softens so does your throat and vice versa. When you are unable to express yourself, your womb and pelvis tighten. Women's voices are meant to moan, sigh, groan, and howl. The more we allow these soundings to move through us organically the more we see the connection between throat, voice, and womb health.

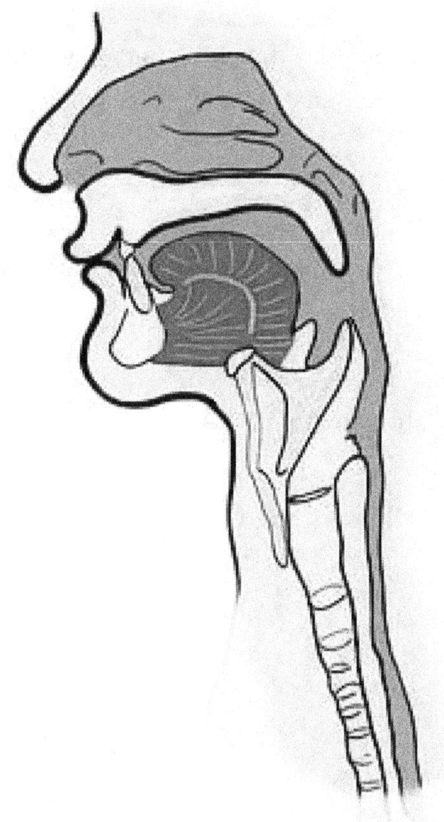

Know the parts of your **throat:**

Epiglottis – keeps food and liquid out of the trachea when we swallow.

Larynx – voice box – produces sound, speech.

Eustachian tube – connects the throat and ear.

Nasopharynx – top of the throat behind the nose.

Oropharynx – middle of the throat behind the mouth.

Hypopharynx – lower part of the throat.

Trachea – tube that carries air between throat and lungs.

Oesophagus – tube that carries food and liquid from throat to stomach.

Hard palate – separates the nose from the mouth.

Soft palate – back of the roof of the mouth.

Lymph nodes – organs that help the body fight infections.

NERVOUS SYSTEM

- The larynx and cervix are connected via the vagus nerve, which when toned regulates our nervous system functions – stress response, sleep, temperature, mood regulation etc.

Voo Sounding Practice

Practice _voo_ sounding daily this month to tone the vagus nerve and activate the parasympathetic nervous system:

➢ Sit comfortably.
➢ Connect to your pelvic floor and throat.
➢ Inhale.
➢ Exhale and sound vooooo.
➢ Repeat five times.

ENERGY: Throat Chakra

Dominant 29–35 years.

The blue wheel and energy vortex located in the centre of the throat. Visualising this supports the energy there to clear and enhance.

Placing your hands on your throat and repeating the mantra, 'I know and speak my truth' and 'I express clearly and with intent' will also support this chakra to strengthen.

Sitting up, place your hands as fists one on top of the other at your womb space – as if you are **holding the dagger of truth of your womb** in your hand with the blade pointing upwards, the tip at your throat. Speak as the blade of truth from your voice.

When in balance this chakra offers us clear communication skills, creative and self-expression.

When out of balance we may experience fear of speaking personal truth, difficulty expressing your thoughts, anxiety or emotional outbursts, sore throat, or mouth ulcers.

The throat chakra is all about mutually affirming communication and truth.

Throat Chakra Opening Practices:

- ➤ Breath out through the mouth, consciously opening your throat.
- ➤ Do gentle neck rolls to relieve tension in the throat area.
- ➤ Journal. To listen to yourself. Ask your womb and voice what it wants you to know daily.

GROUND

Ground your voice and truth.

> ➢ Lie down on your back.
> ➢ Place a grounding cord into Gaia.
> ➢ Extend your neck.
> ➢ Place your Lapis Lazuli crystal on your throat.
> ➢ Inhale.
> ➢ Extend your arms above your head.
> ➢ Exhale.
> ➢ Repeat five times.

ACTIVATE YOUR VOICE

This activity supports you to consciously cultivate your voice. Speaking your truth supports the collective growth of Sacred Womanhood and dismantling of the patriarchy.

Effective communication also enables us to manifest and navigate toxic dynamics.

The first step in activating your voice is waking up to what healthy and unhealthy communication and relationships are.

Healthy and Abusive Relationships

Healthy Relationship	Abusive Relationship
Negotiation and Equality	Coercion and Power Over
Support, Respect and Trust	Isolation, Verbal Attacks and Dismissal
Shared Responsibility and Accountability, Cooperation and Honesty	Denial, Blame and Withholding
Shared Domestic Labour e.g., parenting and Housekeeping. Safety.	Economic Control and Weaponising Children. Unsafe.

Abuse is all about power and control. Abusive methods include:

- Coercion and threat
- Intimation
- Emotional abuse
- Isolation
- Minimising
- Gaslighting
- Use of children
- Male privilege and entitlement
- Economic abuse

There are various types of abuse, including physical, sexual, emotional, psychological and financial.

Effective and assertive communication, alongside boundary setting, are the main components of healthy relationships.

Assertive communication involves maintaining eye contact, speaking in a calm and clear voice, keeping body posture easy, using 'I' statements and holding the space for your own needs, whilst respecting the needs of others.

Aggressive communication involves yelling, eye rolling, 'you' statements, pointing fingers and ignoring the needs of others.

Passive communication involves avoiding eye contact, a quiet voice, collapsed body posture, fear of conflict and ignoring our own needs. Passive-aggressive is a combination of both but also involves outbursts such as slamming doors, gossiping, avoidance, ignoring others or seeking revenge.

Effective communication is rarely modelled to us. We often need support with getting started. **Non-violent communication** is a method, formulated by Michael Rosenberg, which can help us. The template suggests we communicate in this way:

I observe…

I feel…

I need…

My request is…

How to Set Boundaries

Do you know what your boundaries and limits are? Self-awareness and knowing what is and is not ok for you are essential. Boundaries keep us well.

We need to set emotional, resource, energy, time, topic, mental and physical boundaries.

Healthy boundaries are formed from us knowing we are not responsible for saving or fixing others or anticipating their needs. No one has to agree with us, as we are worthy of having our own opinions and feelings. Boundaries mean that we take responsibility for ourselves and needs, which can include making requests of others for support.

When setting boundaries it is useful to assess your capacity, needs, and priorities – and what you consider you will gain from setting the boundary. Making small changes is easier for the nervous system to process. Communicating clearly and frequently with phrases such as 'I will end this discussion if you continue to yell', 'I have one hour to meet for coffee', 'I'm not comfortable with that. If it happens again I will no longer take part', and 'I respect your opinion but am not in agreement'.

Five steps to SOUNDING your Voice and SPEAKING your Truth

Step 1: Know what your truth is

Journal.

What are my previous experiences of speaking my truth?

What have been the consequences?

When do I feel safe to speak? When don't I? Why?

Which boundaries – with whom and where – need to be set?

What would I gain from speaking my truth?

What still needs to be said? To whom?

Step 2: Role play

Have conversations and role play nonviolent communication in a mirror with yourself, with your dog, with your best friend.

Step 3: Step out of your comfort zone

Express your truth in less certain/less predictable situations. REMEMBER to keep regulating your nervous system via the ABC technique [page 62], self-holding, and containment – so that any activation in your nervous system is supported.

Step 4: Strengthen the sound of your voice.

- Complete the vooo womb-throat sounding exercise frequently and the chakra vowels sounds.
- Sing along to your favourite tunes.

Step 5: Improve the clarity and the power of your voice.

- Slow down the pace at which you speak. It gives our voice more authority.
- Record your voice and listen to it.
- Emphasise the pauses in conversations.
- Slow down breathing.
- Allow silence.

Cord Cutting Ritual

Magical Release

Reflect, reassess, and release that which no longer serves.

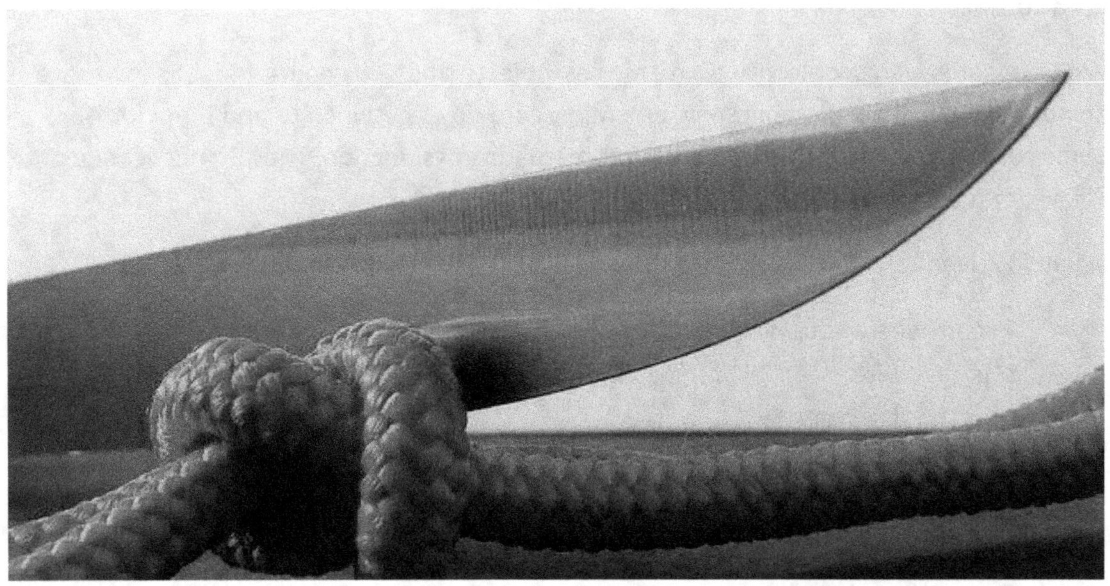

At the festival of Mabon, we connect to the WISE WOMAN. We realise that the answers and guidance we seek are within us. TRUTH is held in the cells of our body, and it is up to us to express and protect this. It is useful to revisit your Life Audit from Ostara. *What has shifted? How do the areas of your life rate for you now? With what or whom do you need to cut the cords with? In which areas of your life or relationships do you need to be more authentic and truthful?*

Ask yourself – *Where do I need support? Where can I get it? Where can I be vulnerable? Who is my trusted circle?*

Sounding your voice consciously and strengthening your boundaries based on your full body 'yes' or 'no' are vital for all Sacred Woman. As you do this for yourself you activate your voice to support the collective to do the same. Challenging patriarchy with your words and truth – and activating your voice in this area – are vital parts of Sacred Womanhood. In addition, so is challenging abuse of all types – to protect the vulnerable, animals and the earth.

Every Last Quarter Moon and/or at the start of your Pre-Menstrual Phase, your Wise Woman is predominant in your energy field. You are strengthened in your inner knowing and ability to see though illusions. Goddess wants you to be infused with fierce boundaries. You can revisit your life audit and see what needs to be released, where you need to ask for help and request that your needs be met. The wise woman and wolf are your allies as you give death to stagnation and blocks in preparation for Dark Moon and bleeding. Cord cutting is a ritual to anchor into your magic toolbox, routine, and monthly planning.

Cord cutting

We form cords with people, places, memories, objects, and behaviours. Indeed, if we have an attachment with or to something, an energy cord flows between us and them (or it). Some cords are unhelpful – draining and perpetuating dysfunction. They do not serve us. These are the cord we need to cut.

What you need:

- A room where you will be undisturbed
- Your favourite essential oils, ideally Frankincense in an oil burner
- Your lapis lazuli crystal
- A candle
- Sage stick for smudging
- Matches
- Fireproof bowl or plate
- Notebook
- Pen

Creating your ritual space:

- Light your candle and oil burner.
- Burn some sage to smudge/energetically clear the area you cord cutting in.
- Make sure you will be undisturbed.

The ritual itself:

- Take three deep breaths. Make sure you are 'in' your body.
- Ground and root yourself into Gaia's womb and connect with your own womb and voice.
- Place your hands, your fingertips, on your throat and womb. Pause and notice the feelings, thoughts and sensations that arise. Infuse your fingertips with the eyes and touch of listening and openness.
- Feel and see if there are any cords in your womb, heart, voice, and mind which are impeding or blocking your creativity, power, love, truthful expression, intuition. You may feel them as hooks or suction.
- Track where they originated – who, what or where are they connected to.
- Prepare to cut these unhelpful cords, knowing that cords of love are eternal and can never be cut.

Then set and speak out loud these intentions for this nurturing ritual:

To reclaim your voice and truth.

To free your power, creativity, love, and intuition.

- Call forth the power of Goddess Morrigan, Earth, Air, Fire, Water, Gaia and the power of your womb, heart, voice, and mind.
- Ask the Morrigan to guide you.
- Place your lapis lazuli in your fingers like a knife/dagger.
- Cut through each cord mindfully and with the intention to free yourself.
- As you do so, say out loud, 'I cut these cords now and liberate myself now, through all timelines, spaces, dimensions and karma.'
- Go slowly, pause if you need to. Less is more. Stop when you feel complete. You can always do this again.
- Complete the ritual. Hold your crystal over your throat and say, 'By the power of the Morrigan I reclaim the truth and voice now'… and then hold the crystal over your womb and say, 'By the power of the Morrigan I free my power, creativity, love and intuition now.'
- Then say, 'It is done' three times… 'And so it is' three times, and then finish by saying, 'This is for the highest good of all.'
- Take three deep inhales and exhales.

When you feel complete, thank Gaia and the Morrigan for their power and support. Perhaps journal about your experience. It may also serve you to write down that which you are releasing on a piece of paper and burn it.

Store your oils and crystal in your cloth magical tool kit bag.

Painting by Kat Shaw

160

KEY CONCEPTS TO INTEGRATE:

DISCERNMENT: sound judgement and assessment.

FEAR: sympathetic nervous system emotional response and sensation.

ANXIETY: sympathetic nervous system emotional response and sensation.

CONTAINMENT: holding difficult aspects of life.

INSTINCT: innate impulse.

INTUITION: internal knowing and understanding without conscious reasoning.

UNDERWORLD: womb of Gaia.

ANCESTRAL: inherited or relating to ancestors.

AWEN: creative inspiration.

MAGIC: influencing mysterious, mystical, and paranormal activities, mystic.

SCRYING: future seeing/telling using a surface.

DIVINATION: seeking insight of the future or mysteries.

THIRD EYE: invisible eye in centre of the forehead giving mystical and spiritual sight / pineal eye.

MYSTIC: someone who directly communicates with the Divine.

WITCH: a woman in her own power who practices magic.

CRONE: wise woman.

SHAMAN: a person who can connect to the Spirit realm, practise divination and healing.

SHAMANIC JOURNEY: setting an intention and entering a meditative journey to receive guidance.

POWER ANIMAL: the energy of an animal you receive into your mind, body, and energy field to guide and support you.

Month: October

Season: Autumn

Festival: Samhain

Direction: South-East

Element: Water

Goddess archetype: MYSTIC and WITCH – The Goddess Cerridwen

Symbol: Eye

Animal: Spider

Moon: Waning Crescent

Menstrual: Pre-menstrual

Body area: Brain, pineal gland, pituitary gland

Chakra: Third eye

Crystal: Fluorite (supports learning, balances energies, protects, stabilises, intuition, universal consciousness).

Oil: Lavender (reduces anxiety, nervous system, self-expression, visualisation).

In this module you will connect with your MYSTIC and your WITCH, your BRAIN, PINEAL AND PITUITARY GLANDS, and your THIRD EYE. They hold the codes and frequency of your INSTINCT and INTUITION. Through these you can practise DISCERNMENT, befriend FEAR and ANXIETY, and journey into the UNDERWORLD to retrieve soul parts and aspects of Self – so that you can expand your wisdom and direct communication with Goddess CRONE and all the sacred supporters who are there to cheer you on.

Your MYSTIC and WITCH also bring you into relationship with your MAGIC and your magical powers which include SCRYING and DIVINATION. In this module you move around your inner world, developing a deeper understanding of the power within you and deepen your understanding of your nervous system and brain. You will learn more about CONTAINMENT and how Goddess, your own Self, can provide a safe vessel for all emotions and sensations to be listened to, felt, learned from, and processed.

The season of Samhain is a time when the veils between the mundane and sacred are thinner and we can 'see' through illusion and dysfunction, and filter through distortion to our own authentic truth.

Connection to your ANCESTRAL patterns and gifts is integral to this module. Through journeying and magical vision, you dig deep into past generation's wisdom and experiences, choosing what to cut the cords with and what to keep. The element of water supports buoyancy on your path and the ability to flow with body sensation and emotional responses. In addition, water supports the cleaning process and dilution of these reactions.

You will also forge links with your inner SHAMAN and experience a SHAMANIC JOURNEY to receive guidance from your inner wisdom and to call in your POWER ANIMAL as support during the winter months.

During this module you become fully conscious to AWEN, creative inspiration, and the relationship between mind and womb, INTUITION, and INSTINCT. The Goddess Cerridwen provides mentorship and a pathway to this.

MYSTIC and WITCH – The Goddess Cerridwen

Cerridwen is the Welsh Goddess of inspiration (Awen), transformation, and rebirth. She is one face of the Dark Goddess, often depicted as a 'hag' and considered to be Goddess of the moon, magic, and the cauldron. She was a mystic, witch, and sorceress, and is a perfect mentor for the season of Samhain.

She gave birth to three children, one daughter Creirwy (Light), and two sons Afagddu (Dark) and Taliesin (a poet).

This Goddess offers us many gifts – predominantly the cauldron of abundance and the blessing of Awen, which is the energy of creative inspiration, prophecy, and wisdom. The main legend about her cauldron involves her son Afagddu and servant boy Gwion. Cerridwen wanted her son to be a seer and set about creating a magical potion to ensure this within her cauldron. This brew needed to be stirred for a year and a day, so she instructed Gwion to do this but to not drink any of it himself. One day the potion bubbled vigorously, and three drops splattered onto Gwion's hand. He licked them and received potent wisdom and power.

The Legend continues with Cerridwen furiously chasing Gwion. During the chase, both continuously shapeshift and metamorphosise. He becomes a hare and she a greyhound, for example. The chase is one of transformation and ends in Gwion being eaten in the form of a grain when she is a hen. The story reader assumes this is the death of the boy but in her belly, he is regenerated and reborn as an inspired, Awen-fuelled poet. Her body, as is ours, is the vehicle for change. We can process the underworld, all emotions, including anger and fear, and change our DNA and ancestral patterns through a metamorphic staged journey.

Cerridwen is aware of the profound impact of cauldron, spells, and elixirs, and teaches us to take our magic and magical tools very seriously. From her we activate our sight, our third eye.

Take a moment to reflect on this and your relationship with magic, death, and transformation. Jot down your thoughts and feelings.

Welcome to October. The season of Indigo. The Earth is preparing for hibernation and so must we. The days of Samhain are the final stages of autumn, and we are moving into the darkest and coldest phase of the year. Lifeforce and sap is returning to the root and into our physical form. Around us we see the barren landscape. All the leaves have fallen, and the weather is cold.

The festival of Samhain falls on the wheel of the year halfway between Mabon and Yule, the Winter Solstice. The calendared date for the festival falls at the end of October and beginning of November. Many associate Samhain with calendared Halloween but the two are in fact different festivals. At this festival there is a recognition of – and the visible connectivity with – death, but it is framed within the trust and faith that through giving death to the old we transform and regenerate and give birth to something new. Samhain is a time for exploration of the MYSTIC and WITCH, internal self-discovery, facing our shadow and challenging body sensations and emotions, which we may have resisted or even feared looking directly at, whilst honouring and trusting our gut instinct.

It is in the dark that we connect to the cauldron of alchemy and metamorphosis. There is a need to descend deep into the underworld, our unconscious mind, and the belly of the earth to retrieve exiled parts and to integrate shadow aspects of self. During Samhain, the veils between the physical and spiritual are very thin. We can access the wisdom of our ancestors and genetic memory. In allowing the renewal of our cells and the releasing of stagnated emotions and energy, the liberation of our ancestral lines can take place. Surrendering into the cyclical nature of life-death-life, trusting and following it whilst allowing the darkness, supports the potency of shamanic journeying, meditation, lucid dreaming, astral travelling, and intuitive knowing.

We explore the landscape of our unconscious and cut the cords with the patriarchal narrative that darkness is evil or terrifying – liberating it and our powerful feelings, where we can discover such wisdom. The rational and logical are not part of this festival. This is the heroine's journey of descent and at the end of it, at Spring Equinox, following the ascent, balance is restored.

At Samhain we receive Awen and discern. We listen and scry, engage in divination work, and connect to the inspired dreams and visions to be birthed during the light half of the following year. At this festival we release and compost, receive and incubate. It is also a great time of year to assess, review and fill the gaps – to learn, find teachers who inspire you. You are PREPARING.

This is the season of the CRONE, the 'elder' of the triple Goddess who remains the dominant feminine energetic through early Winter. The Crone partners with the Shaman, a marriage of masculine and feminine energies, inwardly journeying in union. This is the portion of the year steeped in magic. Alongside Cerridwen, there are many gods and goddesses associated with the festival, including Hecate and Kali. It was in the Middle Ages that the Dark Goddess became depicted and reconfigured as evil. The word Hag in its original form means Holy Woman and they were powerful and revered herbalists, midwifes and oracles of the community. The Christian Church, one of the many patriarchal religions of the world, focused on asserting 'power over' control and dominance, and persecuted and killed hundreds of these women during the Witch Hunt and Trials. In reclaiming the wisdom of the dark, magic, intuitive and mystical arts we resurrect the wisdom of the Crone and exiled aspects of Goddess.

Samhain celebrations can include crystal work, including implanting crystals in the earth, listening to astral meditations, scrying, divination, shadow work, walking alone in the dark at night, connecting to your power animal, and making and wearing masks. Creating a pentacle out of sticks and making a broomstick are fun activities and symbolise clearing energy and setting protective boundaries. Preparing herbal teas to support psychic ability from mugwort (checking any contraindications with medication and do not drink if you are pregnant) are also traditional Samhain rituals.

Purple and black are the key colours of Samhain. Making an ancestor altar with cloths of these colours – adding dried twigs, leaves, stones, candles and photos of your ancestors and a small offering of food to them – is a wonderful way of connecting to their wisdom. Telling the stories of your ancestors, your own life, and the feminine collective with your friends in celebration and reverence of Sacred Womanhood is also an apt activity at this festival.

At this time, we ask ourselves: *What ancestral dysfunction and patterns do I need to clear out of my mind, body, energy, environment, and relationships to create space for MORE and MORE space for my intuition to flourish? What do I need less of?* Conversely, we ask ourselves: *What do I need to invite into my mind, body, energy, environment, and relationships? What do I need more of? What needs to happen for me to reclaim the WISDOM of my sight?*

Our Spider is one of the oldest symbols of the power of the Feminine and her ability to spin and weave fate and the future. The Spider creates the building blocks of life – the threads – and moves with grace and precision to create the cosmic web of all existence. The spider, like the witch and mystic, sees, weaves, and creates strong strands of inspired creative magic. This creature is also intricately linked to the Crone and the Dark Goddess, she who supports us to navigate death – and with calm precision and intention, devours the masculine, the rational and the logic, as the dark half of the year descends. Our spider supports our connection to the mystery and supports our coming into healthy relationship with the shadow aspect of self. She also teaches us patience, receptivity, and the knowing that we weave our own reality.

The ancient symbol of the eye keeps us connected to the sight, coregulation and support of Mother and Grandmother Goddess. In addition, it reminds us of the single spiritual eye we have at the brow point, the third eye, which supports us in our wise, psychic sight, our ability to discern and see the future. The eye of Goddess is the eye of discernment and judgement, of spirit and truth, and so, unsurprisingly, patriarchal societies described it as the evil eye due to their own fear, discomfort, and inability to be with their shadow. The eye, when rotated, takes the almond shape of the vesica piscis, the shape of the vulva, symbolising the creative feminine force and so links the eye, wisdom, intuition, with womb power and instinct. This is the shape of feminine embodied power, intuition, and magic.

What power the wisdom of Sacred Woman has at any age!

Rapid descent happens this month and we are initiated into magic, our underworld, and face the shadows, fear, and anxiety within the mind and body, to be transformed and liberated.

Your Body, Nervous System, and Energy in October

October is the time to connect to your instinct and intuition. To feel, unite and integrate all aspects of your psyche through magical and mystical arts, nervous system regulation – and an interest in the workings of the brain, the pineal and pituitary glands. It is time to deepen your relationship with your nervous system regulatory practises and containment when sympathetic activation of fear and anxiety arise. Your affiliation with your third eye chakra (Anja, which translates as brow, perceive and beyond wisdom) is cultivated this month to deepen your intuition and discernment.

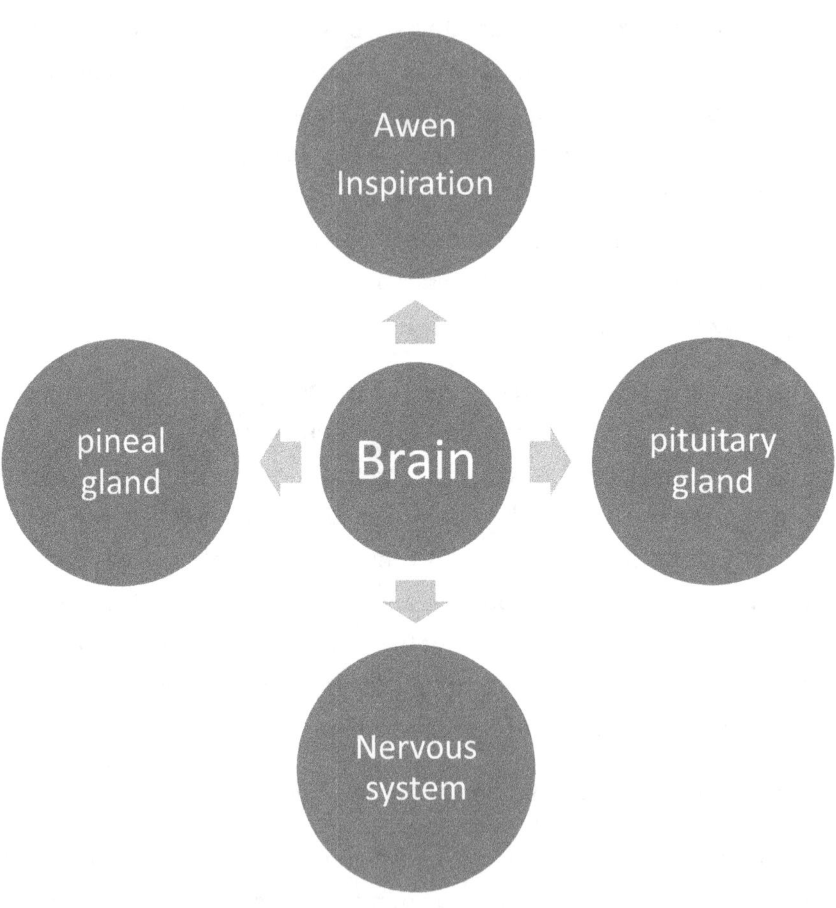

BODY

- Go outside for at least 45 minutes each day.

- Continue to drink plenty of warm fluids but also introduce raw cacao and honey into your daily routine. Eat blueberries and sweet potatoes too.

- Keep a dream diary. What are the dream messages and metaphors? What is the guidance you are receiving?

- Connect to your lavender oil. Diffuse it, add to carrier oil, and massage it into your skin. Ask the scent to support your body to relax so that your inner wisdom becomes stronger.

- Connect to your body weave. Dance like a spider spinning and weaving a web. Imagine you are weaving a new reality or way of being for yourself to be birthed into in the spring.

- Get to know your **BRAIN, PINEAL and PITUITARY GLANDS**.

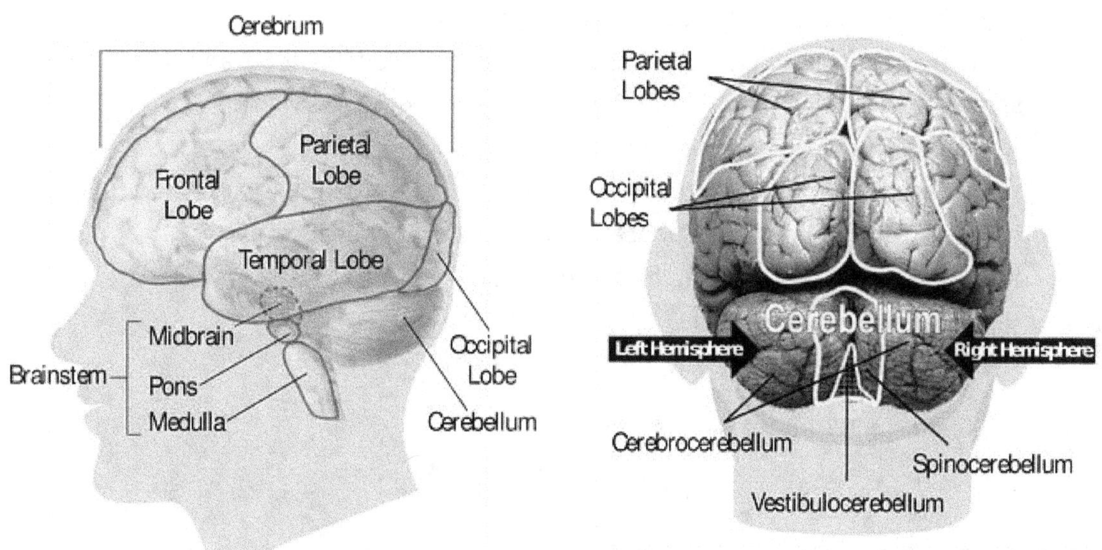

The Brain

The brain is the centre of the nervous system and the most complex organ in our body. The main parts of the brain are:

- **The Lobes:**

  Occipital: supports us to recognise objects. It is responsible for our vision.

  Temporal: responsible for hearing, memory, meaning, and language. They support emotion and learning, interpreting, and processing auditory stimuli.

  Parietal: process nerve impulses (related to the senses, such as touch, pain, taste, pressure, and temperature) and support language functions.

  Frontal: concerned with emotions, reasoning, planning, movement, and parts of speech. Also involved in functions such as creativity, judgment, problem solving, and planning.

- **Cerebral cortex:** controls your thinking, voluntary movements, language, reasoning, and perception.
- **Cerebellum:** controls your movement, balance, posture, and coordination. It is also linked to thinking and emotions. Contains the limbic system ("emotional brain").
- **Hypothalamus:** controls your body temperature, emotions, hunger, thirst, appetite, digestion, and sleep. The hypothalamus is pea sized.
- **Thalamus:** controls your sensory and motor assimilation. Receives and passes on sensory information to and from the cerebral cortex.
- **Amygdala:** regulates your emotions.
- **Hippocampus:** forms and stores your memories (scientists think there are other things unknown about the hippocampus). Also supports learning.
- **Mid-brain:** controls your breathing and reflexes. Includes the Thalamus, Hippocampus, and Amygdala.

The Pineal Gland and Pituitary Glands

These glands are associated with the third eye.

- **Pituitary gland:** controls your hormones and supports many other body functions. It is located at the base of the brain.
- **Pineal gland:** This part controls your growing and maturing. It is activated by light. It is pea-shaped and located in the centre of the brain.

Understanding the Mind

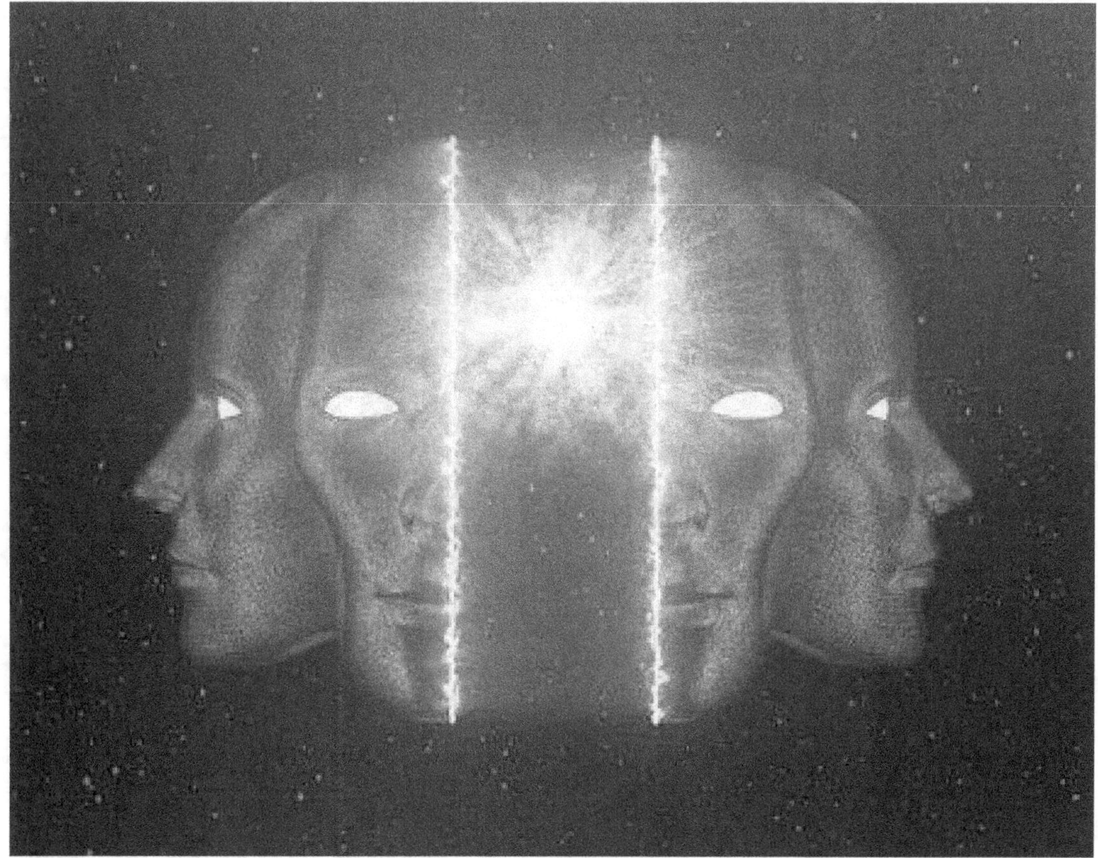

The **Psyche –** all elements of the mind, according to **Freud** – is made up of three parts:

- **ID** – unconscious mind. Impulse. Instinct. Basic needs and desires.
- **EGO** – conscious mind. Arbitrator between id and superego.
- **SUPEREGO** – conscience and morality. Internalised societal norms.

Whereas for **Jung**, the elements of the mind are:

- **Ego** – conscious mind. Persona.
- **Personal Unconscious** mind. Complexes.
- **Collective Unconscious** mind. Archetypes.
- **Self** – whole and unified conscious and unconscious. The totality of the psyche.

NERVOUS SYSTEM

- Do ABC exercise and Containment exercises from the Rainbow Centre Diamond module daily. These support mental and physical health, SAD, restful sleep, nervous system regulation and capacity, turning down sympathetic activation.

Dominant 35-42 years.

The indigo wheel and energy vortex located within the head, at the brow point and within the brain, is the light of the pituitary and pineal glands. Visualising this supports the energy there to clear and enhance.

Placing your hands on your forehead and repeating the mantra, 'I am... I see... I know' will also support this chakra to strengthen.

Addressing identity attachments, how you would complete the sentence, 'I am...' – meditating on the word or adjective you would complete the sentence with, and how it would be for you if you released this identity – is a good practice for activation and exploring the third eye chakra.

When in balance this chakra offers us feelings of clarity, peace, self-awareness, open-mindedness, communication with the spirit and cosmic realms, and expanded consciousness.

When out of balance we may experience disconnect, fear, psychological and emotional distress, headaches, blurred vision, dissociation, concentration issues, mental fog, sleep disorder and stress.

The third eye chakra teaches us that we can trust our instinct, intuition, and inner wisdom – that we are connected and supported by the universe. It helps us to journey into the past and future, retrieving, clearing, and empowering ancestral lines and dysfunction. The third eye offers us faith in our path and inner knowing – and certainty in our decision making.

Experiment with Tapping

Tap on your forehead daily with the intention of activating the Light and Sight of your pineal and pituitary glands.

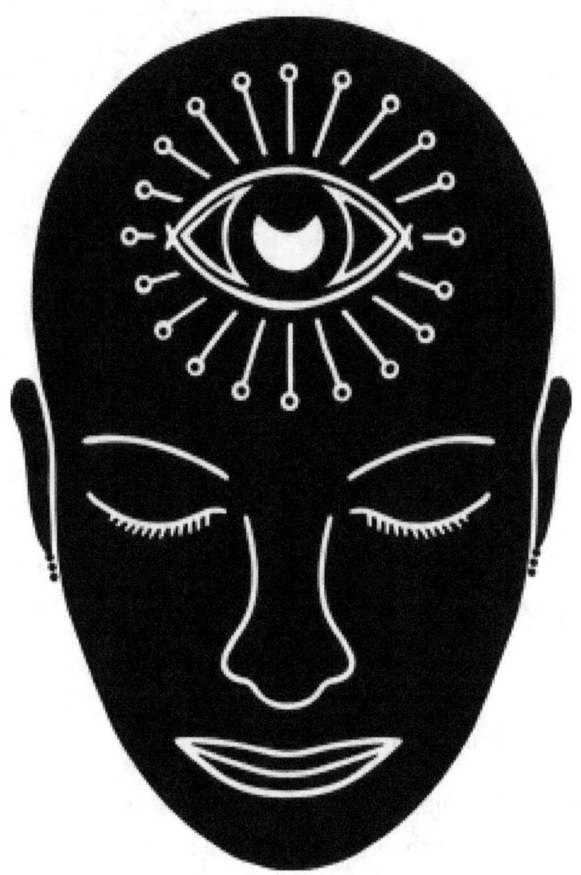

SOUND

Drum, use a rattle or singing bowl (or listen to recordings of these on YouTube or Spotify) to bring your brain waves into the theta state – which helps the third eye open for you to experience a shamanic meditative journeying state.

Speaking/chanting/sounding the word Om… also strengthens the third eye.

GROUND

- Cultivate a grounding and embodied meditation practice in the yoga posture of child's pose to activate your third eye.

Child's Pose for Third Eye Activation

Kneel and sit on your ankles.

Then lean forward, pressing your forehead to the floor.

Bring your breath, intention, and attention to the spot where your brow meets the floor. Breathe in and out from there. Set the intention to open your third eye and see what your inner witch, mystic, crone wants you to see for the highest good of all.

Do this for at least five minutes.

Scrying and Divination

Activate the Witch and her Magic within you.

At the festival of Samhain, we connect to our Mystic and Witch. We realise that we are a cauldron – that we are the body of Goddess – the container of alchemy and magic. We are a cast iron pot, which can securely hold the process of life's difficulties – and the strong feelings, and emotions which accompany them. We can allow even the biggest storm to brew and subside within us. In addition, we realise at Samhain that we are the eye of the storm. We have an aspect of our sight which is clear and is always in direct communication with Goddess. We also make the link between this spiritual intuitive eye and the vital knowledge and insights it receives from the almond shaped vulva and womb space. The seat of our deep instinct. We start to hold ourselves. Contain our nervous system. We start to trust our emotion. We start to LISTEN to our body sensations. We start to stabilise and feel safe – safe enough to weave a new web of reality.

Touching into our inner world and the power of the sorceress, the seer, and the psychic is powerful. Cerridwen mentors us in taking scrying and divination very seriously and to be respectful and clear in our intention around how we use our magical tools.

Claiming and embracing your magic is an act of liberation through all timelines and karma. We honour our female ancestors, the medicine women, midwives, herbalists, and seers who were burned at the stake and support the collective rise of Sacred Womanhood and the Feminine. In doing so, we again challenge the rational, logical dominance of patriarchy.

Going forward throughout the year, every Waning Crescent Moon and/or just prior your menstrual bleed, your Mystic and Witch are predominant in your energy field and your seeress is highly active. She wants you to internally commune – to listen, to release, to integrate – and to self-comfort. She invites you to receive the support of the spirit realm, your spirit guides and animals – and access intuitive guidance about what intentions need to be set during and for the next lunar cycle.

Scrying is a form of divination, where we stare into something to receive shapes, symbols, or visions that we intuitively interpret. It is an act of seeing or peering into the future.

Divination is psychically visioning the future.

There are various tools and forms to facilitate all of this:

1.   Plant helpers and allies

These can amplify your vision, so consider the support of plant medicines. Always investigate thoroughly for any contraindications with medical conditions or medicines you have or are taking. Here are some examples you could research and learn more about:

- Mugwort tea
- Hawthorn tea
- Ceremonial Cacao
- Eucalyptus oil
- Frankincense oil
- Lavender essences
- Lilac essences
- Incense and resins

2.   Methods of Divination

There are many methods and tools for divination. Here are some examples to investigate which may spark your curiosity:

- Tarot
- Oracle cards
- Runes
- Reading tealeaves
- Pendulum work (yes/no)
- Crystal ball or Glass ball reading

- Numerology
- Channelled/automatic writing, sounding, or words
- Scrying

3.   Methods of scrying

Scrying is receiving visions, shape, symbols which we intuitively interpret from a reflective surface or moving element. Examples include:

- Crystal ball staring
- Looking into a fire, scrying into flames
- Cloud scrying
- Sea and wave scrying
- Water scrying with the full moon (in a pond/lake or large bowl of water).
- Black mirror scrying
- Ceremonial cacao scrying
- Bubble bath scrying
- Oil on water scrying
- Rock or stone formation or cracked earth scrying

The options are endless.

At Samhain you can experiment with lots of different types of scrying. And then throughout the year at waning moon – just prior to your menstrual bleed – choose one scrying or divination method to seek guidance through. I would suggest you start by buying your own pack of oracle cards and using them as a divination practice monthly at New Moon. Each pack comes with instructions. Trust your intuition about which pack to buy. There are hundreds of options. Choose a pack which resonates.

Let's try one method of scrying now. Here are instructions on **Water Scrying**.

What you need:

- A large clear glass bowl filled with water
- Your favourite essential oils, ideally lavender
- Your fluorite crystal
- Any other favourite crystals
- Sage stick for smudging
- Matches
- Notebook
- Pen
- Drumming track of music from YouTube.

Scry at night-time, when it is dark, by an open curtained window or outside.

What to do:

- Light your candle.
- Burn some sage to smudge/energetically clear the area you are scrying in.
- Place your crystals around your bowl of water.
- Make sure you will be undisturbed.
- Take three deep breaths. Make sure you are 'in' your body.
- Ground and root yourself into Gaia's womb.
- Place some essential oil on your wrists and inhale deeply.

- Place your hand on your womb and forehead and determine what you would like guidance on. If you are unsure, simply ask what you need to know for the Light half of the year or for the next lunar cycle.
- Call forth the power of Goddess Cerridwen, Earth, Air, Fire, Water, Gaia, and the power of Cerridwen's cauldron, the power of your intuition and womb, and the power of Awen.
- Place your hands in the water and say, 'By the power of the element of water and the Moon I activate my intuitive knowing now.'
- Point your hand to the Sky and say, 'By the power of the air and Awen I activate my higher consciousness and inspiration.'

Play the drumming track. Allowing your brainwaves to change and for you to move into liminal realms.

Soften your gaze and look into the bowl of water. Ask to receiving feelings, visions, symbols, signs, sounds, sensations of guidance.

You will intuitively feel when it is time to complete.

How to complete:

- Hold your hand over your heart and say, 'By the power of my love I thank Cerridwen.'

- Hold your hand over your forehead and say, 'By the power of my sight I thank my intuition.'

- Hold your hand over your womb and say, 'By the power of my womb I thank my instinct.'

- Point your hand at the candle and say, 'By the power of the fire I activate the cleansing flame of change.'

- Point your hand at the earth and say, 'By the power of Gaia I activate the grounding of my intentions into embodiment and manifestation.'

- Then say, 'It is done' three times, and 'So it is' three times, and then finish by saying, 'This is for the highest good of all.'

- Smudge the space again.

Journal your visions and start to form your new intentions for the next New Moon.

Store your oils and crystal in your cloth magical tool kit bag.

Shamanic journeying helps us to gain support and guidance on a specific intention. It is a process of moving beyond the rational and logical and into the liminal and intuitive realms. Below is a meditation which will guide you in a brief shamanic journey to connect you to your power animal. A power animal is an archetypical animal energy which you can activate in your mind, body, and energy field and draw on for guidance, protection, and support. You receive the ability to shapeshift into the skills, qualities, characteristics, and medicine of the animal you connect with.

Preparation:

- Reflect on a behaviour or pattern you see being passed down your ancestral line. For example, a disordered relationship with food, co-dependency, or perfectionism, which you would like more guidance on and to cut the cords with.
- Go to a quiet space where you will not be disturbed.
- Light a candle and smudge the space.
- Breathe fully and deeply. Place in a grounding cord.
- Anoint your forehead with a drop of lavender oil.
- Hold your fluorite crystal in your hand.

The journey:

- Set your intention. *What do you wish to gain clarity and guidance on? What do you want to cut cords with?*
- Clear your mind. Put your hand on your heart. Breathe in and out.
- Play a drumming track.
- Imagine travelling down your grounding cord into the belly of the Earth, the underworld. Notice what the landscape is like.
- Call on your Power Animal. Notice who comes. Thank them.
- Ask them to protect and guide you.
- Ask them to take you on a journey to receive support and guidance on how to cut the cords with the ancestral pattern.
- Watch the journey unfold. Feel, see, know, and receive.
- Travel back up from the earth the way you came.
- Thank your power animal, Gaia, and Spirit.
- At the end, clearly say – I cut the cords with x (speak the pattern you are releasing aloud). Complete by saying 'It is done for the highest good of all.'

Afterwards:

- Journal.
- Smudge yourself and the room.
- You can repeat this journey several times for several issues to gain understanding, release, let go, and cord cut.

Painting by Kat Shaw

Introduction to Violet Module

KEY CONCEPTS TO INTEGRATE:

REST: time out to relax and recover.

WISDOM: knowledge and experience.

TRUTH: own reality, beliefs, and perspective.

GNOSIS: internal knowledge.

IDENTITY: individuality.

TRUST: placing confidence in.

SOVEREIGNTY: power and authenticity, freedom from external control.

BEAUTY WAY: living in harmony.

COMPLETION: process of finishing.

VIRGIN: self-sovereign.

QUEEN: feminine birth right.

DEDICATION: commitment.

Month: December

Season: Winter

Festival: Yule

Direction: North

Element: Earth

Goddess archetype: QUEEN – Goddess Mary

Symbol: Crown

Animal: Owl

Moon: Dark Moon

Menstrual: Bleed

Body area: Hands, Eyes, Nose, Mouth, Ears

Chakra: Crown

Crystal: Amethyst (spiritual awareness, psychic ability, protection, cleansing, inspiration)

Oil: Frankincense (rejuvenates, wellness, immunity, ceremony, peace, satisfaction)

In this module you will connect with your QUEEN and use your fully embodied, five senses to activate SOVEREIGNTY. You come into relationship with your CROWN (the chakra, the top of your head and your physical crown too), along with your HANDS, EYES, NOSE, MOUTH and EARS – portals for your five senses, your QUEEN superpowers, and bodily portals of the Sacred Womanhood experience.

The Dark of this module – Dark Moon, the menstrual bleed, the month of December, and the festival of Yule – are the final training ground, walk-ways, and red carpet to your enthronement. Resilience and faith in your embodied Sacred Womanhood and Light in total darkness are the final challenge and lesson.

Your individual IDENTITY and the MEANING of your life will become clear as you take time to REST and connect to WISDOM (inner and outer) and your own TRUTH and GNOSIS. In doing so, you develop fully your internal locus of control and place your full TRUST in Goddess, inside and out. You initiate as VIRGIN QUEEN – self-sovereign, self-leading, self-referencing – whole and holy unto yourself.

Mother Mary mentors you throughout this module and into COMPLETION and the blessing, bliss, and bounty of the BEAUTY WAY of Sacred Womanhood and the embodied path of living in and through this.

QUEEN – *Goddess Mary*

Mother Mary, Mother of Jesus, has been empowered by several Goddess legends and myths. She is also mentioned in the scriptures of Christianity and Islam. In Europe she is depicted as Black Goddess, the colour of the earthy womb, a totem of fertility. Historical Mary was a Galilean Jew living in Nazareth in the first century. She was the daughter of Anna and Joachim and from the age of three lived in the Temple, preparing for her dedication as an eternal Virgin (she who is complete unto herself). She is a template of rest and receptivity, preparation, and commitment. Mythos suggests that she was fed by Angels, danced, and was trained in Goddess rites and practises. She shows us that we can live in the bliss, abundance, and the beauty way. Her Light conception of Jesus, via her energy and physical body by Spirit, was activated through her agreement and consent – her words 'Let it be' to the Angel Gabriel.

Mary offers us self-sovereignty, trust, and wisdom. She, as the Queen of Heaven (linking her to many other Goddesses, including Isis and Inanna), offers us our throne and crowning as Sacred Women and the pathway to consensual, conscious commitment to our embodiment as the Divine Feminine. She shows us that our locus of control, the compass we need to reference when making decisions, is inside of us. Our truth is internal. She also shows us that we can remain Virgin (complete unto ourselves) whilst also taking on the role of Mother Goddess, the nurturer and Queen, leader, within our family, community, and work.

Finally, Mary connects us to magic, miracles and possibility. Through her own decision-making power, she conceived and gave birth to the Christ energy, love. Without the miracle of her womb, and her voice, her holy yes, humanity would not have known the pure and original teachings of the Christ energy, of love, as they flowed through her son. God is birthed through the body of Goddess. The feminine contains it all. She is known as a meditator or bridge between earth and heaven, lower and upper world, body, and spirit, god and goddess. Mary's body, in particular her womb space, represents fusion, non-dualism, and non-polarity.

Take a moment to reflect on this and your relationship to your miracles and your holy yes.

Welcome to December. The season of Violet. The Earth is quiet, introverted, and internal. Roots are receiving nutrients, strengthening, and preparing. Stabilising is the priority. Externally, there are preparatory signs of the return of the Light as buds are visible. It is cold and dark, and the energy is hardly moving. The Earth is deeply hibernating and in conservation mode. There is a deep period of calm and stillness during the time of this festival. This is a liminal space for even deeper internal journeying and receptivity, gaining insight from the lower and upper worlds.

The festival of Yule, the Winter Solstice, occurs when the wheel of the year pauses again, halfway between Samhain and Imbolc. The calendared dates for the festival are December 20th to 23rd. On this mid-winter's eve, darkness is dominant as we experience the longest night and shortest day. Every part of nature is silent, motionless, suspended. We feel, along with Gaia, cocooned in the womb, preparing for the journey down the miracle and bliss of the red rich velvety menstrual bleed and the birth canal and the manifestation of our visions and dreams. We are fully poised, rested and connected to our internal Self, all of creation, and the cosmos. We are allied and supported in this dreamy state, trusting in the miracle soon to be given life. This is the festival of the QUEEN – of SELF-SOVEREIGNTY, ENTHRONEMENT, AND CROWNING of mind, body, and soul, of IDENTITY, of how we will incarnate in the coming year as Sacred Women. YULE is about our WISDOM AND GNOSIS. The Queen of Heaven and Holy Mother ensures that we use our mind and body in a symbiotic way as the Sun rebirths. We celebrate the active intellect, and our outward self-assertion returns.

The power of incubation and Gaia's darkness are gratefully honoured at this festival as the Sun returns. Our Queen is crowned and enthroned. We have Owl Wisdom – the deep knowing that everything changes, seasons come and go, day turns into night, night turns into day and birth always follows death. We have certainty, confidence, and comfort in all of this. The clarity of our 360-degree vision and absolute faith in our five senses, plus the miracle and sacredness of our embodiment, are vital at this festival as we wake up to the miracle of the union of mind, body, and spirit. This festival is about resting into the trust of our own truth and the paradoxical harmony of completion and change. Excitement can be sensed and yet we now know to pace ourselves and have faith in the intelligence of letting our body lead and bloom in its own time. Gestation and timings are Sacred. We KNOW there is a season and time for everything. We surrender into the trust and faith of the flow of grace.

Our ancestors deeply honoured the potency of the wheel and all it represented at this festival. At Yule, the wheel of time stops turning as Gaia completes her exhale – her release. There is a pause between breaths – the sacred space of anticipation and magic – the absence of everything, the dark cosmic and human womb of potentiality is all that remains – Sophia is here. We and Gaia then inhale again. Light conception happens and rebirth begins. The sun, daylight, and warmth return. The Virgin Mother Goddess rises.

There was great celebration in communities. Fires were lit and the Yule Log, usually of oak, the tree connected to the sun god, was burnt ritually, marking the oak king's triumph in the battle of the oak and holly kings at this solstice. The smoke from the log cleared the home from darker energies and blockages so the new energy could be invited in. Candles were a big part of this festival, also symbolising the return of life and the sun. This festival, as at Litha, merges polarity, simultaneously looking backwards and forwards, celebrating the full expansion of the inner, of darkness and death, whilst recognising the return of the outer, light and life. Our circular vision and step into timelessness as the wheel of the year pauses, frees us from the concept of linear time, and moves us into the eternal now. We receive the certainty that personal, ancestral and collective lines can be altered and changed at any given moment. We are constantly in Cerridwen's cauldron of regeneration in the dark half of the year and as Queen can be supported by any of the Goddess mentors to release, reconfigure and rebirth. We remember in our DNA what our ancestors revered and knew – that there is no differentiation between us and Gaia. We are the Triple Goddess; Virgin/Maiden in Spring, Lover/Mother/Warrioress in Summer, and Wisewoman/Crone in Winter and at Summer and Winter Solstice we are unified – Queen of Earth and Heaven – as one. We are all parts of Goddess, and how we express this is unique to us. It is our IDENTITY.

The homes of our ancestors were adorned with evergreens, such as holly, ivy, mistletoe, and the bows of sacred trees such as yew. The wheel was honoured by placing the evergreen wreaths on the door. There would be gatherings, candle lit processions and celebrations with carolling and feasting with lanterns and a table decoration honouring the wheel of the year and the four directions. Smoke was a symbol of the mystery of the phoenix rising and our ancestors would join with their family, in gratitude, dancing around the fires and bathing themselves in the smoke of the oak fires to smudge and cleanse their energy and physical form. There would be legend and storytelling and sharing throughout the night, dance and they would await and celebrate the sunrise, often making a commitment or intention or 'resolution' to ensure that the Light they have conceived is birthed into form.

This month we ask ourselves: *What are we conceiving? What blocks to me attaining my intentions do I need to release?* Conversely, we ask ourselves: *What do I need to invite into my mind, body, energy to expand and make space for growth? What do I need more of? What needs to happen for me to follow and trust my 360-degree vision and wisdom?*

Our Owl is a symbol of the Lunar Feminine, of Wisdom, of intuition and our ability to see in the dark. Her circular vision means we can see completely – in all directions and perspectives – and then tune into our internal gnosis and truth to weigh it all up and decide what is right for us. She is a totem of midwifery and will support us in birthing that which we conceive with the grace and ease of her winged flight. In addition, the Owl helps us to connect to Awen, inspiration, and internal guidance – helping us see beyond illusion, masks, and deceit – and explore magic, change, and transitions with grace and ease. She is the faithful ally of the Queen and supports our self-sovereignty and the opening of SIGHT.

The ancient symbol of the crown is representative of authority, divinity, and sovereignty. It is the talisman of royalty, leadership, and dedication to service. The wearer is enthroned in their own wisdom and union with the Divine, the sacred marriage of heaven and earth, humanness, and divinity. The sanctity of womanhood. Crowns also symbolise glory, immortality, empowerment, and initiation. Stepping into the rulership of the Soul.

What a miracle a Sacred Woman is!

As at Litha, socialising, celebrating, and performing are activities of this month. Indoor fires further fuel our expression fires and joy. Love and gratitude for your community, singing and chanting together in union strengthens bonding. Making an altar, decorating with evergreens is a beautiful focus for working with intention setting. Lighting candles to invite the Light to kindle the flames of your desires is also a beautiful way of strengthening resilience and trust in cosmic support.

Most of all, we need to become focused and ensure our will is clearly aligned with our intentions and goals and that those we are in alliance with are serving our highest good and manifestation. This month is about cultivating and strengthening the power of the alignment of mind and body.

Your Body, Nervous System, and Energy in December

December is the month to conceive. To expand and fully activate your super senses, touch, taste, sight, hearing, and smell. To become super sensitive and ready. To trust your bodily messages and wisdom. To receive a multidimensional experience. To receive the solar rebirth, cosmic and heavenly energy, a deep penetrative activation through your hands, nose, eyes, ears, and mouth. It is time to deepen your relationship with your blood and unconscious, it is time to see the Light in the Darkness and the wisdom it all. It is the month to come into relationship with your crown (Sahasrara, which translates as a thousand petaled) to commune with and as the Queen of Heaven, as Divine awareness, and the full embodiment of Soul.

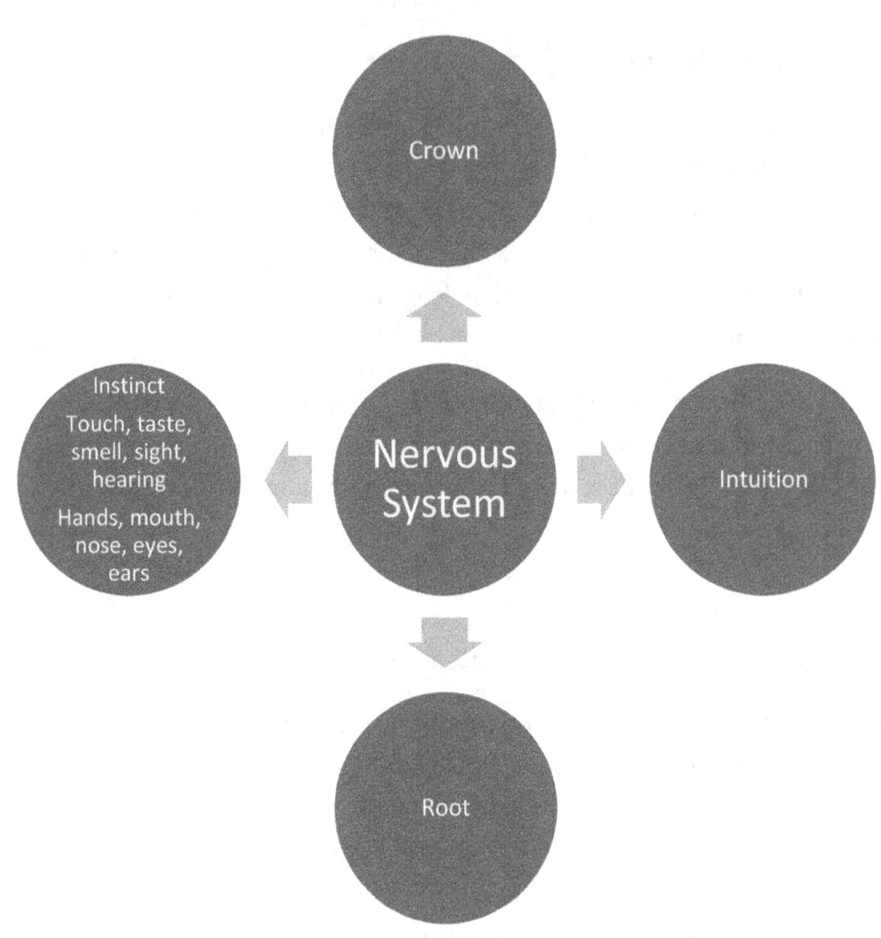

Crown
Instinct
Touch, taste, smell, sight, hearing
Hands, mouth, nose, eyes, ears
Nervous System
Intuition
Root

BODY

- Go outside for at least 30 minutes each day.

- Continue to drink plenty of fluids, increasing your intake of chamomile tea and plain hot water.

- Mix some of the frankincense essential oil with a carrier oil, such as fractionated coconut oil, and massage some at the base and top of your spine and the crown of your head. This will ground, stabilise, and motivate your crown chakra to open all at the same time.

- Connect again to your menstrual blood. Touch it, smell it, and look at it intensely. Your blood will speak to you about your Self, your life meaning and identity. Learn from it.

- Do a crystal breathing meditation.

Light a candle and smudge the space you are sat in.

Sit on the floor crossed-leg, in easy pose.

Feel your perineum against the floor. Put in a grounding cord.

Place your hands on your lap palms up.

Place the amethyst crystal on the crown of your head.

Inhale and exhale through the top of the head, imaging the crown opening and closing for ten breaths.

Feel your perineum against the floor again.

Open the crown and call on the rainbow light.

Receive.

- Make a self-leadership and sovereignty playlist of your favourite female artists. Listen to it and sat on your throne, wearing your crown.
- Connect to your five senses fully. Cook a meal for yourself mindfully. Feel the sensation of textures of the food through your hands as you prepare it, connect to the smells fully, the colours, the cooking sounds. Take your time to set a beautiful table. Consciously and slowly taste the first mouthful of food. Give thanks to your five senses.

Get to know all the vehicles of your five senses. Your HANDS, EYES, EARS, NOSE and MOUTH – all parts.

Hands. Fingers to grip and grasp. Palm, back (with veins), wrist connecting hands to arms and enabling movement.

Eyes. RETINA – picks up images and discerns colour. IRIS – coloured part, regulates how much light enters the eye. LENS – small part around the centre of the eye. Controls focus. PUPIL – centre of eye, dilates depending on how much light the eye is in contact with. CORNEA – layer that covers the eyes. It allows light to pass. SCLERA – white area around the iris, lens, and pupil. OPTIC NERVE – connects the eye and brain.

Ears. Outer ear – has three sections: pinna or auricle – on outside of our heads, channels sound and vibrations, ear canal – tube that helps sound to move inside the ear, eardrum – fragile thin sheet which vibrates when the sound hits it. The middle ear – air and three bones in it – the hammer (malleus), anvil (incus), and stirrup (stapes). They amplify sound. The inner ear – fluid and the cochlea. This translates sounds into electrical signals for the nerves to message the brain, via tiny hairs that vibrate with the sound waves in the fluid. Also supports balance.

Nose. Two holes called nostrils. The nostrils and the nasal passages are separated by the septum which is made of thin bone close to your skull, and flexible cartilage at the tip on the face. Behind your nose is a middle space called the nasal cavity, connected with the back of the throat. Inside of your mouth the palate separates off the nasal cavity.

Mouth. Lips – entrance to the mouth, are made of skin, muscle, and mucous membranes, which allow opening and closing and speech. The hard palate at the front separates the mouth from the area of the nose and the soft palate keeps food and drink from going down the airway instead of the oesophagus. The tongue is a muscle of the mouth. Helps the forming of sounds and tasting foods. The gums, cover the jawbone and protect the teeth.

NERVOUS SYSTEM

Visualise the kundalini energy – the double helix of the DNA – the two serpent streams of light moving from the earth through the perineum, coiling around your backbone and spinal cord, twisting, and turning to create energy and flow and then out through your crown in a cascading waterfall of energy.

Then rest.

Take some time out to rest fully. Switch off. Have no agenda. Just be.

Tune into your nervous system. *What does it need from you this next year?* Set some intentions around inviting in calm, safety, and regulation around your daily practises.

ENERGY: Crown Chakra

Dominant 43-49 years.

The violet wheel and energy vortex located within the area of the crown at the top of the physical head.

Placing your hands on your head and repeating the mantra, 'I am peace. I am supported. I listen to myself. I am Goddess. I am one with the universe' will also support this chakra to strengthen.

Standing up and placing the arms and hands above the head in a funnel shape will help you channel and connect the rainbow bridge of light.

When in balance this chakra offers us connection to the support of the cosmic realms and universal energies, connection to soul, easy access to our internal wisdom and sovereignty, serenity, pace, wholeness, completion, and access to 360-vision, the ability to see the bigger picture. We will trust, flow, and stay present.

When out of balance we may experience depression, aloneness, dissociation, disconnectedness, and lack of compassion and empathy. We may feel apathy, boredom, have an inflated ego, or have fatigue and headaches.

The crown chakra reminds us that we belong and are supported, that we are interconnected. It reminds us that we are both Goddess and supported by Goddess. It connects us to cosmic consciousness and the mind of the cosmos. In addition, a balanced crown chakra allows us to observe our thoughts from our wisdom seat, like an owl.

Experiment with channelling rainbow energy through your crown.
Breathe in through your feet and the top of your head. Consciously notice that as the breath passes through the soul star chakra it helps to create a ball of energy there.

Lift the ball of energy out of the soul star chakra. Lower and stretch it into a halo around the top of the head, opening a portal ring.

Call in the rainbow spectrum of light. Feel its arrival. Direct your consciousness to travel up it and move along the rainbow. See what is at the end. Ask to be shown how you are to incarnate and what your identity is for the coming year.

You cannot get this wrong. Goddess knows how to mentor you in this empowerment energy channelling. Invite Mary to journey with you.

GROUND

- Mindfully walk daily. Explore the beauty way of deep winter – what do you see, hear, touch, and smell. *Does the air have a taste?*

- Earth is the predominant element. Place your hands on the soil, dig some up. Look at it closely, smell it deeply. This is the body and peak time of the Dark Divine Feminine.

- Go on a nature walk. Ask to see an owl. Ask to find a black feather. Also watch for synchronicity and signs as to how Goddess is communicating with you.

At the festival of Yule, we connect with our QUEEN. We realise the POWER of GNOSIS and INTERNAL TRUTH and SELF-SOVEREIGNTY. We are everything and as such are VIRGIN, whole and holy unto SELF. Our body is the portal of MAGIC and MIRACLES.

Consciously knowing we have eyes to see in the Dark supports us to feel protected and fear less. In the blackness of Dark Moon and the final moment before our menstrual flow our inner-knowing and truth is fully revealed. We KNOW our truth. Our instinct guides us. Our menstrual blood is the red carpet to our Queen throne – we initiate every month and rebirth through it.

Claiming Queendom, self-sovereignty, self-referencing, and self-leadership is a political act. You are free from the matrix and control of the external trends, paradigms, thoughts, advertising, and commercialism. You are whole and holy unto Your SELF. Your SELF gives your life meaning and Your SELF is your truth and identity. You complete yourself.

Every Dark Moon and/or at the very onset of your Bleed, your Queen and Owl are predominant in your energy field, and your dominion, sovereignty and self-trust are highest. They want you to be infused with your crown, and to create a beautiful space to sit in and be in the world – radiant, self-sufficient, and enthroned. Rededicating to your own truth, to

Self and tuning in and totally trusting in your own Wisdom are your magical actions at this time of the month.

Creating your Throne, Altar, and Crown

Choose a spot for your throne and altar. Ideally this is a place in nature which is beautiful and undisturbed or is a tidy corner of the room with a chair and table or tray.

What you will need:

- A large piece of cloth – any colour or design
- A stone or crystal of each colour – diamond, white, red, orange, yellow, green, blue, indigo, violet
- Candle
- Sage stick for smudging
- Matches
- Oracle cards if you have some
- Items for your **altar**
    - A tray
    - Some flowers and foliage and herbs
    - A shell
    - A stone you have found
    - A feather
    - A handful of soil
    - Any other objects, statues, pictures, photos you find beautiful, or which have a spiritual significance to you
    - Your wand
    - Items to make your crown
    - Paper crown: paper, scissors, Sellotape, stapler, glitter, sequins, coloured pens, and pencils
    - Evergreen/Flower: Floral wire, scissors, greenery, flowers

How to create your beautiful magical space to enthrone and crown yourself as Queen:

- Burn some sage to smudge/energetically clear the area you have chosen.

- Make sure you will be undisturbed.

- Take three deep breaths. Make sure you are 'in' your body.

- Ground and root yourself into Gaia's womb and through your crown connect with the energy of the Mary, Queen of Heaven, and your Owl.

- Call forth the Goddess, the directions of the north, south, west, and east and the elements of Earth, Air, Fire, Water, Gaia, and Sophia, the power of your mind, your intuition and your womb, your creativity, and the power of Eros and Awen.

- Create your altar first. On the tray, create the four directions, place the soil (EARTH) at the top in the north, candle (FIRE) at the bottom in the south, shell (WATER) to the left in the west, and the feather (AIR) to the right in the east. In the centre place the flowers and herbs to represent Lifeforce. You can place any other objects you would like on the tray too. Hold your wand over the altar, light the candle, and say, 'I activate this sacred space of harmony, the beauty way.'

- Create your throne. Unfold your cloth (going forward you can store your crystals and wand in it) and place it on your chair or the ground. Hold your wand over the cloth, and say 'I activate this throne, the seat of my self-leadership.'

- Create your crown. Hold your wand over the crown and say, 'I activate this crown with self-sovereignty – I am the ruler of my own life.'

- Sit on your throne and crown yourself. Tune into your womb, heart, and mind to receive guidance with the support of Mary and your Owl. Write down anything that you receive. Draw some oracle cards. Ask yourself *'what is my truth?'* and *'what do I need to know about myself as Queen?'*

- Listen to yourself.

- Complete by giving thanks to Goddess, the directions of the north, south, west, and east and the elements of Earth, Air, Fire, Water, Gaia, and Sophia, the power of your mind, your intuition and your womb, your creativity, and the power of Eros and Awen. End by saying, 'Blessed be' three times.

Once completed, safely store your crystals and wand in your cloths. Your altar can be taken apart or permanently kept. You can renew it or make a new one for each festival, changing the colours of the objects or flowers on it. You can dedicate it to an intention.

You can sit on your throne whenever you need to tune into yourself and receive inner guidance and place the crown on your head to feel sovereign.

It is all your choice. You are the magic.

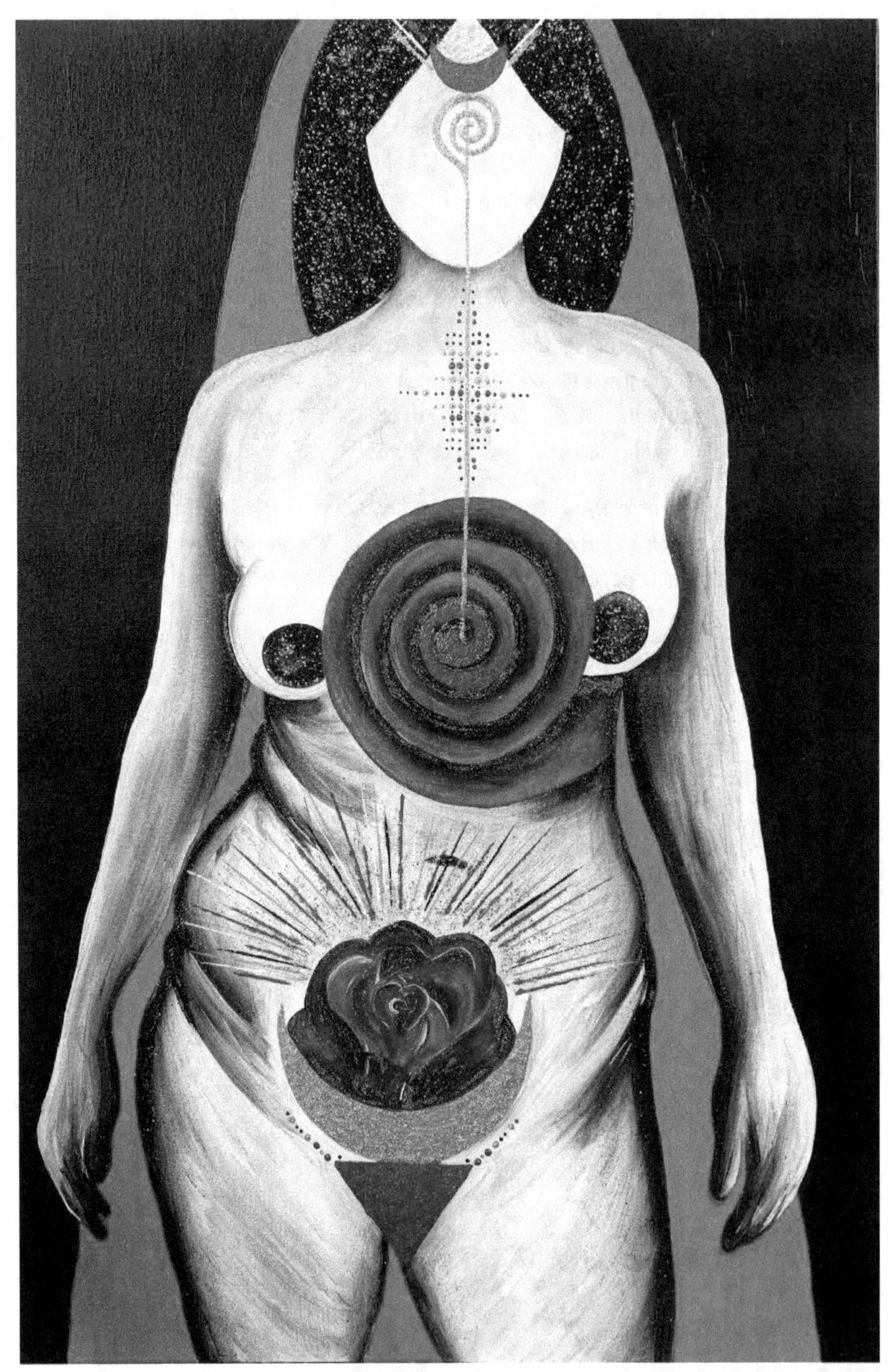

Art by Kat Shaw

Initiation and Dedication Ceremony

I congratulate, bow down and honour you. You have completed all the modules and are now ready to initiate and dedicate yourself to Sacred Womanhood.

You will need:

- A large piece of cloth – any colour or design. You choose.
- A shell
- A stone or crystal of each colour – diamond, white, red, orange, yellow, green, blue, indigo, violet
- All your other crystals
- Candle
- Sage stick for smudging
- Matches
- Your crown
- Your wand

In preparation you need to:

- Complete the crown, throne, and altar activity.
- Ensure you will not be disturbed during the initiation and dedication ceremony. You will need approximately 1.5 hours.
- Have written a list of nine words, representing your key learning from each Goddess mentor in each module.
- Have written three sentences, which are pledges or promises of how to live your life as a Sacred Woman.

Your Dedication and Initiation Ceremony:

- Burn some sage to smudge/energetically clear the area you are doing the ceremony in.
- Make sure you will be undisturbed.
- Take three deep breaths. Make sure you are 'in' your body.
- Ground and root yourself into Gaia's womb and through your crown connect with the energy of the Earth and Heavens.
- Lay out cloth to create your throne.
- Place your crystals in a circle around the cloth. Say, 'I sit on the throne of the beauty way.'

- Call forth the power of Goddess, the four directions, North, South, East, and West, the four elements, Earth, Air, Fire, Water, Gaia, Sophia, Spirit and the power of your womb, heart, and mind.
- Place your crown on your head and say, 'I now declare myself Queen of Heaven, Earth, and my Body. I am one with Gaia and Sophia. I am self-sovereign woman.'
- Use your wand to cast a magic circle of protection – trace the circle of crystals with your wand and say, 'I cast a circle of life and protection around me by the power of Goddess.'
- Place your wand on your womb and think about your first promise. Connect to your body. Hold your hand over your womb and say, 'By the power of my blood I activate my first pledge…' Say it aloud.
- Place your hand on your heart and think about your second promise. Connect to your body. Hold your wand over your heart and say, 'By the power of my love I activate my second pledge…' Say it aloud.
- Hold your wand over your forehead and say, 'By the power of my sight I activate my third pledge…' Say it aloud.
- Point your wand to the Earth and say, 'By the power of Earth I initiate and dedicate into Sacred Womanhood with the blood, lifeforce, eros and Dragon power of the earth.'
- Point your wand to the Sky and say, 'By the power of the Air I initiate and dedicate into Sacred Womanhood with the consciousness, inspiration and power of the air.'
- Point your wand at the candle and say, 'By the power of Fire I initiate and dedicate into Sacred Womanhood, lighting the flames of passion, power and magic within me.'
- Point your wand at the shell and say, 'By the power Water of I initiate and dedicate into Sacred Womanhood supported by the flow and change.'
- Then say, 'It is done' three times and, 'So it is' three times, and then finish by saying, 'This is for the highest good of all.'
- Thank each of the Goddess mentors in turn – saying their names and what you learnt from them.

    Gaia
    Sophia
    Brigid
    Aphrodite
    Athena
    Mary Magdalene
    The Morrigan
    Cerridwen
    Mary

Cheer, celebrate. Take time to feel into how you are different and how you will live your life as a Sacred Woman moving forward.

Think about how you will serve the Feminine, Goddess and Woman.

Congratulations. Thank you for taking this journey. May all you have learnt, discovered, and recovered serve the highest good of all and the rising of the Feminine and remembrance of Goddess.

Further Exploration: A Growing Sacred Womanhood Resource List

Understanding the Nervous System: Irene Lyon https://irenelyon.com and Kimberly Ann Johnson https://kimberlyannjohnson.com

Understanding Energy: Donna Eden https://edenenergymedicine.com

Self-Compassion: Kristin Neff https://self-compassion.org

Menstrual Cycle: Alexandra Pope and Sjanie Hugo Wurlitzer https://www.redschool.net

Vulva: Samantha Zipporah https://www.samanthazipporah.com/mappingtheyoniverse

Goddess: https://www.thegirlgod.com

Goddess Art: Kat Shaw https://katshaw.art

Mentorship with Goddess Private Facebook Group:
https://www.facebook.com/groups/mentorshipwithgoddess

You can find a **Tool Kit** for this workbook at http://thegirlgod.com/mentorship_toolkit.php.

Girl God course offerings, including the year-long Mentorship with Goddess Programme, can be found at https://thegirlgod.com/courseofferings.php.

Images
All art and photographs belong to Kat Shaw, Kay Louise Aldred, or public domain (free and royalty free stock from https://pixabay.com/) unless otherwise noted.

Cover art by Kat Shaw / katshaw.art

Acknowledgements

Heartfelt thanks and appreciation to **Trista Hendren** for saying yes to this project and her continual cheerleading, enthusiasm, and expert editing – which she effortlessly does alongside her amazing mum, **Pat Daly**, for whom I am also grateful. A huge thank you also to **Kat Shaw** for saying yes to her art being used for the cover of this book – this was a huge honour, and the image, for me, is a perfect depiction of a Sacred Woman. I would also like to thank her for letting the book showcase her art throughout.

In addition to Trista and Kat and all those I collaborate with at Girl God Books, I would like to acknowledge and honour my Goddess mentors **Achintya Devi**, **Ameya Cohen** and **Lynne Sedgmore** who have steered and guided me over the last couple of years. Thank you.

A special thanks also to **Sue Ellen Parkinson** whose service to and channelling of the Magdalene energy through art has been deep source of inspiration to me and food for my soul.

Thank you to all of the sacred women I am in community with at **The Acorn Wellness Retreat**.

I'd like to acknowledge the learning I have received from the **hundreds of teenagers and young women** I have had the honour to teach and work with pastorally throughout my career. This book is for you and the **many women** I have mentored, coached, and facilitated workshops and retreats for over the last few years.

My deepest love and gratitude to my daughter **Elizabeth** for being the muse and motivation for this book and to my husband **Dan**. I could not do this work without his love, support, and encouragement.

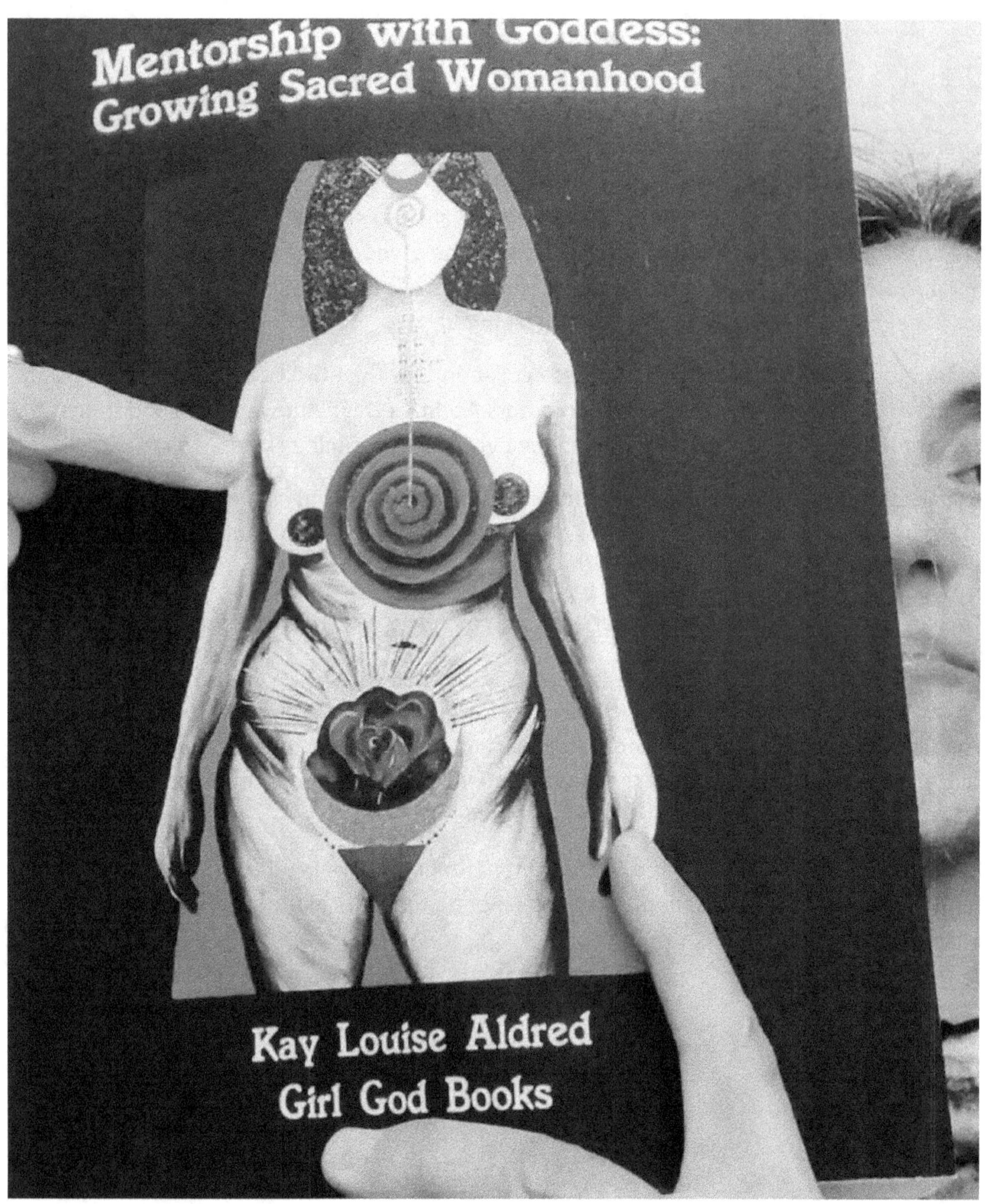

If you enjoyed this workbook, please support the author and our small independent press by writing a brief review on Amazon and/or Goodreads!

We LOVE photos of our readers with Girl God Books! Please post on social media to spread the word – or email them to support@girlgod.org.

What's Next?!

Making Love with the Divine: Sacred, Ecstatic, Erotic Experiences – Kay Louise Aldred

Somatic Shamanism: ***Your Fleshy Knowing as the Tree of Life*** – Kay Louise Aldred

The Crone Initiation: Women speak on the Menopause Journey – Edited by Kay Louise Aldred, Trista Hendren, and Pat Daly

Rainbow Goddess – Celebrating Neurodiversity – Edited by Kay Louise Aldred, Trista Hendren, Tamara Albanna and Pat Daly

Pain Perspectives: Finding Meaning in the Fire – Edited by Kay Louise Aldred, Trista Hendren and Pat Daly

Embodied Education: Creating Safe Space for Learning, Facilitating and Sharing – Kay Louise Aldred and Dan Aldred

Kali Rising: Holy Rage – Edited by C. Ara Campbell, Jaclyn Cherie, Trista Hendren, and Pat Daly

Songs of Solstice: Goddess Carols – Edited by Trista Hendren, Sharon Smith, and Pat Daly

Goddess Chants and Songs Book – Edited by Trista Hendren, Anique Radiant Heart and Pat Daly

Heart to Heart: Words from Goddess/Divine Feminine Wisdom – Kat Shaw

Imperfectly Fabulous – Kat Shaw

Out of Darkness She Speaks: A Rich Anthology of Poetry and Artwork Inspired by the Feminine – Leonor Murciano-Luna, PhD

Anthologies and children's books on the Black Madonna, Mary Magdalene, Mother Mary, Cerridwen, Aradia, Kali, Brigid, Sophia, Spider Woman, Persephone, The Old Antlered One/Ancient Deer Goddess, An' Cailleach and Hecate are also in the works.

Details to be announced.

http://thegirlgod.com/publishing.php

www.ingramcontent.com/pod-product-compliance
Lightning Source LLC
LaVergne TN
LVHW060336200726
843506LV00008B/530